Approachable Accessibility

Planning for Success

Martine Dowden
Michael Dowden

Apress®

Approachable Accessibility: Planning for Success

Martine Dowden
Brownsburg, IN, USA

Michael Dowden
Brownsburg, IN, USA

ISBN-13 (pbk): 978-1-4842-4880-5
https://doi.org/10.1007/978-1-4842-4881-2

ISBN-13 (electronic): 978-1-4842-4881-2

Managing Director, Apress Media LLC: Welmoed Spahr
Acquisitions Editor: Louise Corrigan
Development Editor: James Markham
Coordinating Editor: Nancy Chen

Cover designed by eStudioCalamar

Cover image designed by Freepik (www.freepik.com)

Distributed to the book trade worldwide by Springer Science+Business Media New York, 233 Spring Street, 6th Floor, New York, NY 10013. Phone 1-800-SPRINGER, fax (201) 348-4505, e-mail orders-ny@springer-sbm.com, or visit www.springeronline.com. Apress Media, LLC is a California LLC and the sole member (owner) is Springer Science + Business Media Finance Inc (SSBM Finance Inc). SSBM Finance Inc is a **Delaware** corporation.

For information on translations, please e-mail rights@apress.com, or visit http://www.apress.com/rights-permissions.

Apress titles may be purchased in bulk for academic, corporate, or promotional use. eBook versions and licenses are also available for most titles. For more information, reference our Print and eBook Bulk Sales web page at http://www.apress.com/bulk-sales.

Any source code or other supplementary material referenced by the author in this book is available to readers on GitHub via the book's product page, located at www.apress.com/9781484248805. For more detailed information, please visit http://www.apress.com/source-code.

Printed on acid-free paper

In loving memory of Dr. René and Dr. Josette Ebtinger whose research and compassion helped make a better world for children everywhere.

Table of Contents

About the Authors

 **Martine and Michael Dowden** are cofounders at Andromeda, FlexePark, and M2D2 Enterprises. Together they leverage a combined 40 years of experience in tech and education to build accessible software products and educate others on UX, design, and development topics. Martine uses her degrees in psychology and visual design to create beautiful web interfaces that are usable by everyone. Michael uses his education in computer science and entrepreneurship to build software and businesses that are ethical and inclusive.

About the Technical Reviewer

Katherine Joyce is a passionate designer and developer with over 7 years of experience having worked across the financial and government sectors. She creates innovative, intuitive customer experiences and is an advocate of accessible design. As Lead UX/UI Designer at Alt Labs, she is leading the UX vision and crafting beautiful solutions driven by user needs. In her previous role, she worked as a Senior UX/UI Designer for Accenture promoting accessible design in government services and helping automate legacy processes to improve the customer journey. She has also spent over 5 years with AXA Insurance as an Application Support Software Developer where she fixed bugs in legacy financial systems, debugged issues with browser compatibility, and suggested improvements to customer-facing journeys. She is passionate about advocating accessible design and mentoring those who would like to have a career in design or development.

Acknowledgments

Writing a book is a project of passion and commitment and takes a tremendous amount of time and support from friends and family. We would like to thank our children, Brook and Xander, for their patience during this process, and of course their grandparents, Marc and Elisabeth Ebtinger, and their aunt and uncle, Ariaunah and Vincent Ebtinger, for making it possible for us to dedicate time to writing and conferences.

We wouldn't be here today if it weren't for our years of engagement with the community, which started at the Code PaLOUsa software development conference. Our extreme thanks to the organizer Chad Green for taking a chance on having us at his conference, and for years of friendship. His commitment to ethics and inclusivity and the welcoming environment at his conference have been appreciated by our entire family.

Of course, our work on accessibility did not spring fully formed from nothing. Early influences include Elle Waters and Nat Tarnoff, whom we first met at Code PaLOUsa and later at the Midwest UX conference. Another special thank you to Kit Wessendorf who worked closely with Martine for 2 years on a major accessibility project.

There's one person that stands alone as the single catalyst that made this book possible. The remarkable Philip Japikse, an international speaker who has written several books for Apress, has been tremendously influential in helping develop our accessibility practice. Our many thanks to Philip for making this possible. We must also thank the wonderful team who produced our first book: Alex Papadimoulis, Patrick Roach, and Rachel Govert who were a joy to work with.

Finally, we must mention those who contributed directly to the pages you're about to read. The Apress team of Louise Corrigan, Nancy Chen, James Markham, and Katherine Joyce has been supportive the whole way, from walking through the proposal process to ensuring the quality of the finished book. Our last thanks to Léonie Watson, Lainey Feingold, and Nate Parker who went above and beyond to support our research on the history of accessibility and the people involved.

CHAPTER 1

Why Should I Care About Accessibility?

The purpose of web accessibility is to remove barriers and bring the information, services, and functionality of the Web to as many people as possible so they can be included in this global community. Similarly, the goal of this book is to make the subject of web accessibility approachable to technology professionals who work on web sites, and web and mobile applications.

In this first chapter you will find a definition of accessibility, along with a description of people impacted by these topics.

Web Accessibility

When the World Wide Web was invented by Sir Tim Berners-Lee[1] in 1989, the goal was to connect people and information in an open and accessible way. So when the World Wide Web Consortium (W3C) launched the Web Accessibility Initiative (WAI) just 8 years later, Berners-Lee had this to say:

Worldwide, there are more than 750 million people with disabilities. As we move towards a highly connected world, it is critical that the Web be usable by anyone, regardless of individual capabilities and disabilities.[2]

---

[1]Photo: Sir Tim Berners-Lee at #WebWeWantFest, by Belinda Lawley – https://flic.kr/p/pr3PZw.
[2]Press Release: W3C Launches Web Accessibility Initiative, www.w3.org/Press/WAI-Launch, accessed October 24, 2018.

M. Dowden and M. Dowden, *Approachable Accessibility*, https://doi.org/10.1007/978-1-4842-4881-2_1

While the Web has brought us a never-ending ocean of information, services, and cat memes, granting us the ability to connect with others on a global scale, with unprecedented speed, this is not the case for everyone. As of 2011, the World Health Organization (WHO) reported over 1 billion individuals with disabilities, representing 15% of the global population. This number is continually on the rise due to an aging population, an increase in chronic health conditions, and improvements in measurement methodologies,[3] increasing the need to create a more accessible Web for all.

Sadly, the popular press typically reports that over 95% of all web sites are not accessible to users with disabilities.[4] Research on web accessibility challenges has determined that developing countries, in particular, suffer from lack of awareness, resources, and training related to accessibility.[5]

Awareness of accessibility and its demands is lacking among those designing and implementing web sites. There is a corresponding scarcity of developers, testers, and designers familiar with accessibility testing. One reason is a shortage of books, courses, and training materials on accessibility that are available to web development teams. And even when the team knows what they need to do, often resources allocated by the companies involved are insufficient.

Because such a large percentage of sites are not designed with accessibility in mind, access to entire categories of information or services may be totally out of reach for many users. Equal access to information, a basic human right as described by the United Nations in section 21 of the Convention on the Rights of Persons with Disabilities (CRPD),[6] becomes even more paramount when looking at global statistics of said individuals regarding health, economic status, and education, all of which show disenfranchisement.[7] As a populace it is our ethical obligation to make sure that the technology we produce does not contribute to or further the disadvantages the disabled community already faces.

---

[3]"World Report on Disability," World Health Organization, October 16, 2018, `www.who.int/disabilities/world_report/2011/report/en/`, accessed October 24, 2018.

[4]Sullivan, Terry, and Rebecca Matson, "Barriers to Use," Proceedings on the 2000 Conference on Universal Usability – CUU 00, 2000, doi:10.1145/355460.355549.

[5]Abuaddous, Hayfa Y, Mohd Zalisham Jali, and Burlida Basir, "Web Accessibility Challenges," *International Journal of Advanced Computer Science and Applications* 7 (10)2016: 172–81.

[6]"Article 21 – Freedom of Expression and Opinion, and Access to Information," United Nations, `www.un.org/development/desa/disabilities/convention-on-the-rights-of-persons-with-disabilities/article-21-freedom-of-expression-and-opinion-and-access-to-information.html`, accessed October 24, 2018.

[7]"World Report on Disability," World Health Organization, October 16, 2018, `www.who.int/disabilities/world_report/2011/report/en/`, accessed October 24, 2018.

What Is Web Accessibility

In the context of the Web, being accessible means that the web site or application is designed and implemented in a way that people with disabilities can also use it. More specifically, that they can perceive, understand, navigate, interact, and contribute to the Web.[8]

When reading about accessibility you will commonly see it written as **a11y**. This is a numeronym, where the letters between the first and last are replaced by a number which represents the count of letters removed. This numeronym is sometimes used as a substitute for the word "accessibility," but for readability it is recommended to use the full word "accessibility" in place of the numeronym whenever possible.[9]

There are many factors to consider when thinking about accessibility, including the content, browsers, assistive technologies, users, developers, and tools related to the web site. All of these are interconnected and must work together in order to achieve an end product that will be accessible and usable.[10,11]

Content

When considering content in the context of accessibility we need to look at more than just the words on the page. Content encompasses images, forms, videos, and all other pieces of the application that convey information to the user. Content also reaches beyond the rendered items to include the code and markup that generates and displays the information being consumed by the user.

Technology

The choice of technology stack, authoring tools (such as for blogs and content management systems), and libraries used to author the application coupled with engineering team's experience with the stack, accessibility guidelines and standards,

---

[8]"Introduction to Web Accessibility," Web Accessibility Initiative, www.w3.org/WAI/fundamentals/accessibility-intro/, accessed October 24, 2018.

[9]https://a11yproject.com/posts/a11y-and-other-numeronyms/.

[10]"Essential Components of Web Accessibility," W3C Web Accessibility Initiative (WAI), www.w3.org/WAI/fundamentals/components/, accessed October 29, 2018.

[11]"Accessibility Principles," W3C Web Accessibility Initiative (WAI), www.w3.org/WAI/fundamentals/accessibility-principles/, accessed October 29, 2018.

and browsers or user agents to be supported can make a big difference in development effort. Furthermore, some libraries and frameworks already have accessibility support built-in, but others do not, which leads to greater development efforts and possible needs for work-arounds.

Browsers and user agents such as desktop graphical browsers, mobile phone browsers, multimedia players, and other technologies used to deliver the content have many similarities but also many differences. An understanding of which ones will be used is critical for both those developing and those testing as what may work in one browser may not in another.

End User

While one goal of web accessibility is to ensure everyone is able to navigate and read information, the demographic and experience of the end user will impact the overall usability, and therefore the overall accessibility. For instance, the user's knowledge of the topic being presented, and comfort with the relevant technology, will help determine design patterns to make sure the application is fully usable.

Evaluation tools and user testing help determine if the application is, in fact, usable and accessible for the target audience.

Disabilities

So how do we make sure we are good stewards of the Internet and contribute to its movement toward being the great equalizer it is promised to be? First, let us define some terms to ensure we are speaking the same language. Disability, impairment, and handicap are often used interchangeably in everyday vernacular, but each has a distinct meaning.

An **impairment** is a loss of (or an abnormality of) function or structure of mind or body. The impairment may therefore cause a **disability** which is the restriction or prevention in performing an action. The **handicap** is the disadvantage that the disability causes for the individual in performing tasks.[12,13]

---

[12]"Disabilities," World Health Organization, October 05, 2017, `www.who.int/topics/ disabilities/en/`, accessed October 24, 2018.

[13]Department of Public Health, University of Liverpool, "Impairment, Disability, and Handicap," 819.

For example, a macular abnormality such as cataract (an impairment) may cause blindness (a disability) which may prevent the person from enjoying a book or driving a car (handicap).

For ease of discussion we have grouped disabilities into six general categories: auditory, visual, physical, cognitive, neurological, and speech. The reality, however, is that disabilities are not this cleanly delineated and will often include aspects from multiple categories.

Auditory

Fifteen percent of the world's population experiences some kind of hearing loss. Around 466 million people, or 5% of the world's population, have disabling hearing loss (loss in the better ear greater than 40 decibels for adults, or 30 for children). By 2050, this number is estimated to grow to over 900 million people, or 10% of the population. A demographic of note are those over the age of 65, one-third of whom are currently affected.[14] Causes include exposure to loud noises, genetics, injury, age, and illness.[15]

An auditory disability can range from significant hearing loss in both ears, or deafness, to mild hearing loss in one or both ears. Individuals may be able to hear sounds but may have difficulty understanding speech if it is unclear or distorted, or subject to a lot of background noise. Users with auditory disabilities often rely on any combination of the following to access audio information:

- Transcripts or text alternatives which provide the same information as the auditory track

- Captions or subtitles which synchronously provide a text alternate for both speech and nonspeech audio information

- Extended audio descriptions which are added to media by pausing the video to allow for time to provide description where dialog or narration pauses are too short but context or information would be lost without extra audio description

- Sign language interpretation

---

[14]"Deafness and Hearing Loss," World Health Organization, www.who.int/news-room/fact-sheets/detail/deafness-and-hearing-loss, accessed October 29, 2018.

[15]"Causes of Hearing Loss in Adults," American Speech-Language-Hearing Association, www.asha.org/public/hearing/causes-of-hearing-loss-in-adults/, accessed October 30, 2018.

- Options on media players to pause, stop, increase or decrease delivery speed, and adjust volume

- Options on media players to change caption fonts, font size, and color to make reading easier for the user

- Clear audio tracks so that speech can be easily understood

They will struggle if these are not provided or if interactions with the application rely on voice controls only.[16]

Visual

Visual impairments vary from mild to substantial uncorrectable vision loss in one or both eyes. Around 1.3 billion people globally have some form of vision impairment.

In order to access information online, visually impaired users will use text-to-speech, speech-to-text, customize settings for fonts, colors, and spacing, screen magnification, listen to audio descriptions, or use refreshable braille. But in order for these technologies to function, code design must follow specific guidelines for the assistive technologies to be able to render or speak the content.

The leading causes of visual impairment and blindness are shown in Figure 1-1,[17] with descriptions following.

---

[16]"Diverse Abilities and Barriers," W3 Web Accessibility Initiative, www.w3.org/WAI/people-use-web/abilities-barriers/, accessed October 30, 2018.

[17]"Consultation on Public Health Management of Chronic Eye Diseases Report of a WHO Consultation," www.who.int/blindness/publications/CONSULTATION_ON_CHRONIC_EYE_DISEASES.pdf?ua=1, accessed November 13, 2018.

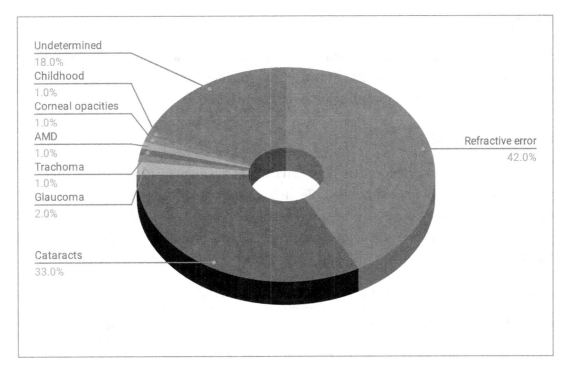

Figure 1-1. *Leading causes of visual impairments and blindness*

Refractive Errors

Refractive errors encompass nearsightedness, farsightedness, and curved corneas causing distortion. As of 2010 this was the cause of visual impairment in 101.2 million people and blindness in 6.5 million people worldwide.[18]

Cataract

Cataract is a clouding of the lens of the eye which prevents clear vision. As of 2010 this affected 20 million people globally and was responsible for 51% of the world's blindness.[19]

---

[18]Hashemi, Hassan, et al., "Global and Regional Estimates of Prevalence of Refractive Errors: Systematic Review and Meta-Analysis," *Journal of Current Ophthalmology*, vol. 30, no. 1, 2018, pp. 3–22, doi:10.1016/j.joco.2017.08.009.

[19]"Priority Eye Diseases: Cataracts," World Health Organization, www.who.int/blindness/causes/priority/en/index1.html, accessed November 13, 2018.

Glaucoma

Glaucoma is a group of diseases characterized by damage to the optic nerve caused by an increase of fluid and pressure in the eye.[20] An estimated 4.5 million individuals are affected by glaucoma accounting for just over 12% of blindness worldwide.[21]

Color Blindness

Another form of visual impairment that often leads to the inability to interpret content visually on the Web is color blindness, affecting around 8% of males and 0.5% of females. Color vision happens because the eye processes light through three different types of cones. These cones allow us to determine color.[22] Table 1-1 lists several types of color blindness.[23]

Table 1-1. *Color Blindness Classification and Statistics*

Classification	Description	Type		Male	Female
Trichromacy	Anomalous trichromacy	Normal color vision. Uses All three types of light cones.		92%	99.50%
Anomalous trichromacy	Use all three cones but one cone is faulty	Protanomaly	Reduced sensitivity to red	1%	0.01%
		Deuteranomaly	Reduced sensitivity to green	5%	0.40%
		Tritanomaly	Reduced sensitivity to blue	Rare	Rare
Dichromacy	Two types of cones	Protanopia	Unable to perceive red	1%	0.01%
		Deuteranopia	Unable to perceive green	1.5%	0.01%
		Tritanopia	Unable to perceive blue	0.008%	0.008%
Monochromacy/ achromatopsia	No color	See only shades of gray from black to white		Rare	Rare

[20]"What is Glaucoma?", American Academy of Ophthalmology, `www.aao.org/eye-health/diseases/what-is-glaucoma`, accessed November 13, 2018.

[21]"Priority Eye Diseases: Glaucoma," World Health Organization, `www.who.int/blindness/causes/priority/en/index6.html`, accessed November 13, 2018.

[22]Kalloniatis, Michael, "The Perception of Color," Current Neurology and Neuroscience Reports, July 09, 2007, `www.ncbi.nlm.nih.gov/books/NBK11538/`, accessed November 13, 2018.

[23]"Types of Colour Blindness," Colour Blind Awareness, `www.colourblindawareness.org/colour-blindness/types-of-colour-blindness/`, accessed November 13, 2018.

Physical

Physical disabilities may include limitations of movement, mobility, dexterity, or stamina. Causes can include muscle weakness including tremors, lack of coordination, paralysis, numbness or diminished sensation, joint disorders, hampered movement, or missing limbs. There are a multitude of causes of physical disability, examples include amputation, rheumatism, injury, or disorders such as muscular dystrophy or fibromyalgia.

Access to web content is impeded for individuals with physical disabilities, often due to challenges with a mouse or touch display. Providing full keyboard support is important both because it is more accessible for some users and also because other assistive technologies depend upon the same focus and navigation techniques commonly implemented for keyboard. Usage challenges can be compounded when insufficient time is provided to complete the task or if page's function and navigation controls are not clear and predictable.

There are a wide variety of devices created to aid individuals with physical disabilities ranging from ergonomic keyboards to mouse-like devices, head pointers, joysticks, sip-and-puff devices, eye tracking, and many more. To ensure that users can access the content with their preferred technology, keyboard support, large clickable areas, and visible indicators of the current items in focus are very important. Also important are keyboard shortcuts and the ability to type them in sequence, as some users may not be able to type the key combinations simultaneously. Many of the requirements for web content to be accessible to users with physical disabilities overlap with those for cognitive and visual disabilities.

Cognitive and Neurological

Neurological disorders are diseases of the central and peripheral nervous systems. The central nervous system is composed of the brain and spinal cord while the peripheral nervous system encompasses the nerves and ganglia that are not part of the brain or spine.

Cognition is the activity of thinking, understanding, learning, and remembering.[24] There is not a perfect overlap between cognitive and neurological disabilities. It is important to note that cognitive disability is not synonymous with decreased intellectual function and that many individuals with cognitive impairments do not have any intellectual function limitations.

---

[24]"Cognition," Merriam-Webster, www.merriam-webster.com/dictionary/cognition, accessed October 29, 2018.

A common cause of cognitive and neurological disability is dementia, a major cause of disability in older populations affecting around 50 million people worldwide or 5–8% of individuals over the age of 60.[25] Other causes include epilepsy (affecting over 50 million people worldwide), illnesses (bacterial, viral, and fungal alike) such as meningitis or zika, trauma, strokes, or Parkinson's disease (affecting over 10 million people worldwide[26]).[27]

Barriers to accessing information for individuals with cognitive or neurological impairments include complex or confusing navigation and content structure. Therefore, clearly structured, consistent content with predictable behavior is paramount. Simple text accompanied by illustrations and graphs to visually convey the information being presented is also very helpful.

Also a consideration is blinking, flashing, or flickering images or media, or audio tracks, playing in the background that cannot be turned off.

Flashing or flickering content is especially problematic for individuals with photosensitive epilepsy, a condition, affecting 3% of epileptics, that triggers seizures when exposed to flashing lights. Known triggers are television screens and computer monitors with flickering or rolling images. Although triggers vary by person, generally lights flashing at a rate of 5 to 30 flashes per second are most likely to trigger a seizure.[28]

Depending on their needs, people with cognitive or neurological disorders may use a variety of web browsing methods including text-to-speech, captions, or speed controls to increase or slow down the rate at which information is being presented. These overlap with the accessibility requirements for auditory, physical, speech, and visual impairments depending on the method.

---

[25]"Dementia," World Health Organization, www.who.int/en/news-room/fact-sheets/detail/dementia, accessed October 30, 2018.

[26]"Statistics," Parkinson's Foundation, www.parkinson.org/Understanding-Parkinsons/Causes-and-Statistics/Statistics, accessed October 30, 2018.

[27]"What Are Neurological Disorders?", WHO, www.who.int/features/qa/55/en/, accessed October 30, 2018.

[28]"Photosensitivity and Seizures," Epilepsy Foundation, www.epilepsy.com/learn/triggers-seizures/photosensitivity-and-seizures, accessed November 19, 2018.

Speech

Speech disabilities include the inability to pronounce or enunciate speech that is recognizable by others or by voice recognition software.[29]

Users with speech disabilities will struggle with interfaces that require voice commands. This includes web sites that only have a phone number to contact the site administrators. Alternative means of communication or interaction are necessary such as a keyboard alternate for voice commands or a chat option or contact form instead of phone number only.

The three most common speech disorders are detailed as follows.

Apraxia of Speech

Apraxia occurs when neural pathways used to control speech muscles do not function properly.[30] The person may know what they want to say but are unable to articulate it. Apraxia is typically caused by strokes, dementia, brain tumors, or traumatic brain injuries.[31]

Stuttering

Stuttering, also known as stammering, is a form of disfluency typified by verbal blocks, prolongations, and repetitions making it difficult to speak clearly or rapidly. This also includes vocal tics which are the involuntary production of sounds or movement such as throat clearing or palilalia (repeating one's own words).[32] The exact cause is unknown.[33]

---

[29]"Diverse Abilities and Barriers," W2C Web Accessibility Initiative, www.w3.org/WAI/people-use-web/abilities-barriers/#speech, accessed November 18, 2018.

[30]"10 Most Common Speech-Language Disorders," Speech Pathology Graduate Programs.org, www.speechpathologygraduateprograms.org/2018/01/10-most-common-speech-language-disorders/.

[31]"The Five Most Common Speech Disorders in Adults," Raleigh Capitol: Ear, Nose, & Throat, www.raleighcapitolent.com/blog/speech-disorders?entryid=98&tabid=89, accessed November 18, 2018.

[32]"Motor and Vocal Tics," Cedars-Sinai, www.cedars-sinai.edu/Patients/Health-Conditions/Motor-and-Vocal-Tics.aspx, accessed November 18, 2018.

[33]"The Five Most Common Speech Disorders in Adults," Raleigh Capitol: Ear, Nose, & Throat, www.raleighcapitolent.com/blog/speech-disorders?entryid=98&tabid=89, accessed November 18, 2018.

Dysarthria

Dysarthria is a speech disorder caused by nerves or muscles involved in producing speech such as the diaphragm, lips, tongue, or vocal chords. This can lead to slurred or slowed speech, limited range of motion of the tongue, jaw, or lip, difficulty articulating, and many other symptoms.[34] Examples of causes include brain tumors, Lou Gehrig's disease, and Parkinson's disease.[35]

Diversity of Abilities

While accessibility is extremely important for those with permanent disabilities, the principles of accessible web sites and applications benefit everyone. Due to the tremendous diversity of internet users, there are vast discrepancies in situation, skills, expectations, tools, and ability. Even those who are not considered disabled may find themselves in circumstances where they depend upon accessibility for a period of time, or even simply for convenience. Consider these three scenarios:

- **Temporary disability:** A person who has broken their glasses and therefore magnifies the text on their screen to find the nearest optician. This user is temporarily disabled by their broken glasses, and they benefit from accessibility features while they are waiting for their glasses to be replaced.

- **Situational limitations:** Someone who is sitting in a very crowded and noisy subway station trying to watch a video on their phone suffers from situational limitation. They turn on the captions because they can't hear the video's sound track due to the background noise. This person is not disabled but is limited by their situation and therefore benefits from accessibility features.

---

[34]"10 Most Common Speech-Language Disorders," Speech Pathology Graduate Programs.org, www.speechpathologygraduateprograms.org/2018/01/10-most-common-speech-language-disorders/.

[35]"The Five Most Common Speech Disorders in Adults," Raleigh Capitol: Ear, Nose, & Throat, www.raleighcapitolent.com/blog/speech-disorders?entryid=98&tabid=89, accessed November 18, 2018.

- **Age related**: An elderly individual is trying to call their grandchild for their birthday. Because they can't remember the phone number or how to use the phone app, they use voice assistant to "Call grandchild on cell."

In all three of these cases we have users that don't consider themselves disabled but because of their current situation benefit from accessibility features. In other cases, a user may have multiple disabilities and rely on a wide variety of features in order to interact with the Web. It is therefore important to design and architect for a wide variety of needs rather than to categorize by pathology or medical classifications.

Assistive Devices, Features, and Techniques

Individuals with disabilities use a wide range of devices[36,37] and techniques to interact with applications on the Internet, whether by customizing their settings on their machines or by utilizing specialty hardware or software. These can be categorized into two different types of approaches:

- **Assistive technologies:** Software and hardware such as screen readers, screen magnification software, or refreshable braille displays used to improve interaction with the Web.

- **Adaptive strategies:** Techniques such as increasing text size or turning on captions to improve interaction with the Web. These can be done with both mainstream hardware and software or with specialized technologies.

While assistive technologies are chosen by a user to help with their specific challenges, it is important that our web sites and web applications correctly support these tools to maximize access and usability.

Tools and preferences used can be grouped into four main categories: Perception, Presentation, Input, and Interaction.

---

[36]"What Are Some Types of Assistive Devices and How Are They Used?", NIH, www.nichd.nih. gov/health/topics/rehabtech/conditioninfo/device, accessed November 18, 2018.

[37]"Assistive Technology Devices," Georgia Department of Education, www.gpat.org/Georgia-Project-for-Assistive-Technology/Pages/Assistive-Technology-Devices.aspx, accessed November 18, 2018.

Perception

Perception has to do with our senses. For the Web this includes auditory, tactile, and visual. A user who has limited ability with a sense will use their other senses to compensate. Furthermore, some disabilities will require users perceive information using multiple senses in order to understand it, such as reading along while text is being read to them. Some tools and techniques include the following.

Auditory

Tools and techniques related to the accessibility of content meant to be heard.[38]

 Captions are a synchronized transcript of the auditory portion of videos, often displayed over a portion of the image. Captions often include nonverbal information, such as indicating when background music is playing. Like captions, subtitles are frequently used to translate dialog into another language.

Transcripts are a complete textual representation of the entire content of an audio file (or video) including description. This is certainly helpful for those who are hard of hearing, but also allows you to catch up on your favorite podcast while on the plane.

Visual and tactile notifications, such as blinking lights or vibrating phones, have become common. We use these technologies when in very noisy (or perhaps in very quiet) environments. Taken even further, haptic technology can provide very detailed feedback to the user, even making buttons on a flat touch-screen device feel real.

Visual

Tools and techniques related to what can be seen include refreshable braille displays,[39] such as the one pictured here. They represent content being displayed in braille by raising and lowering pins, updating as the cursor moves on the page (Figure 1-2).

---

[38]https://commons.wikimedia.org/wiki/File:Closed_captioning_symbol.svg.
[39]Photo: Mobile Braille-Leiste für 7.000, by Stefan Evertz – https://flic.kr/p/6cGow9.

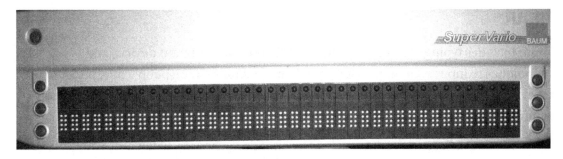

Figure 1-2. *Refreshable braille display*

In addition to visual notifications, vibration or other tactile feedback may be used along with an audible alarm or ringtone. Videos may be produced with audio descriptions, which is an audible narration of the visual components.

Screen readers have become a ubiquitous accessibility tool, with one or more free versions available for every major platform, typically bundled with the operating system. This is software that converts content on the page to speech (or braille). They often provide extra shortcut key combinations to expand navigation capabilities of content via the keyboard.

Presentation

One way to improve accessibility is to allow users to choose how content is presented to them. These configurations may be provided by the operating system, browser, or application.

Allowing a user to customize fonts and colors can make text easier to read. This can be any combination of font size, color, typeface, or spacing. It is also important to have good defaults, and that the user interface that provides configuration is itself accessible and easy to read.

Screen magnifiers are also helpful in making text more accessible. They are typically able to increase the size of text, or even entire sections of the screen to make it easier to see. This may be either a hardware or software feature.

Anytime audio or video is presented in an application it should be easy to mute or pause the media, as well as providing volume controls so that the media can be adjusted separately from system sounds.

Pop-up and animation blockers give users control over distractions and effects that can be disorienting or confusing.

Input

Input includes typing, writing, and clicking.[40] People use different devices and techniques to input content or interact with applications. Some people may prefer to use a keyboard over a mouse or vice versa, while others might prefer a different device or type of interaction entirely. Examples of devices and tools include

- Specialized keyboards such as ergonomic keyboards, keyboards with larger keys, different spacing, illuminated keys, or custom layouts

- Mice, trackballs, joysticks, touchpads, and pointer devices

- On-screen keyboards and touch-screens

- Sip and puff devices (Figure 1-3) where movement is controlled via the tube like a joystick and clicking is accomplished by inhaling or exhaling through the tube

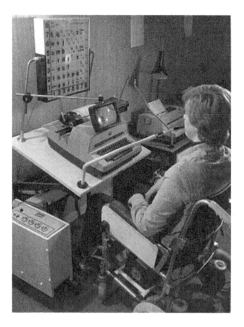

Figure 1-3. *Sip and puff device*

- Voice recognition software that uses human voice to control the computer or program

- Eye tracking systems that register eye movement to control the mouse pointer, using blinks for clicks

- Spelling and grammar tools such as spellcheck

- Input filtering software that recognizes and filters out involuntary movements

Interaction

Interactions refer to how the user navigates through, and locates content in, an application or web site. There are a number of features and strategies that can make this easier for any user.

Content should have clear hierarchy including titles, headings, and labels that are descriptive. Links, buttons, and controls should have consistent and predictable labeling and positioning. Feedback messages, whether communicating an error, success, or additional information, are easy to read, descriptive, and in plain language.

Multiple navigation mechanisms should be provided, such as sitemaps, breadcrumbs, or search functionality, in addition to primary navigation. Providing skip links to allow keyboard users to bypass repeated blocks of content (such as headers or primary navigation) allows them quicker access to primary content.

All existing browser features should be supported by every web site or application. This means back and forward buttons should always navigate as expected. Additionally, all pages should have clean, navigable URLs supporting bookmarking for easy access in the future.

Summary

This chapter introduced you to the fundamentals of web accessibility, as well as an overview of the millions of people impacted by accessibility features every single day (including you). Now you know

- The difference between impairment, disability, and handicap

- Examples of disabilities that may prevent full access to the Web

- Reasons accessibility is important, even for those who are not considered disabled

- Various tools that are available to help manage limitations of access

In the next chapter you will learn about the history of web accessibility and the people and organizations that help bring web content and functionality to all.

CHAPTER 2

The Road to Accessibility

This chapter builds upon what you have learned about web accessibility in Chapter 1, by discussing the people, organizations, and standards that are leading us to a universally accessible Web.

Accessibility Timeline

Consider a future device ... in which an individual stores all his books, records, and communications, and which is mechanized so that it may be consulted with exceeding speed and flexibility. It is an enlarged intimate supplement to his memory.[1]

—Vannevar Bush, 1945

The concept of the Internet as we know it today can be traced back to 1945 in Vannevar Bush's article advocating for making knowledge more accessible, a theme that will continue throughout the development of the Web and still reverberates today. The timeline of accessibility starting from this point is illustrated in Figure 2-1, highlighting major milestones along the way.

---

[1]"As We May Think," *The Atlantic*, www.theatlantic.com/magazine/archive/1945/07/as-we-may-think/303881/, accessed December 8, 2018.

© Martine Dowden and Michael Dowden 2019
M. Dowden and M. Dowden, *Approachable Accessibility*, https://doi.org/10.1007/978-1-4842-4881-2_2

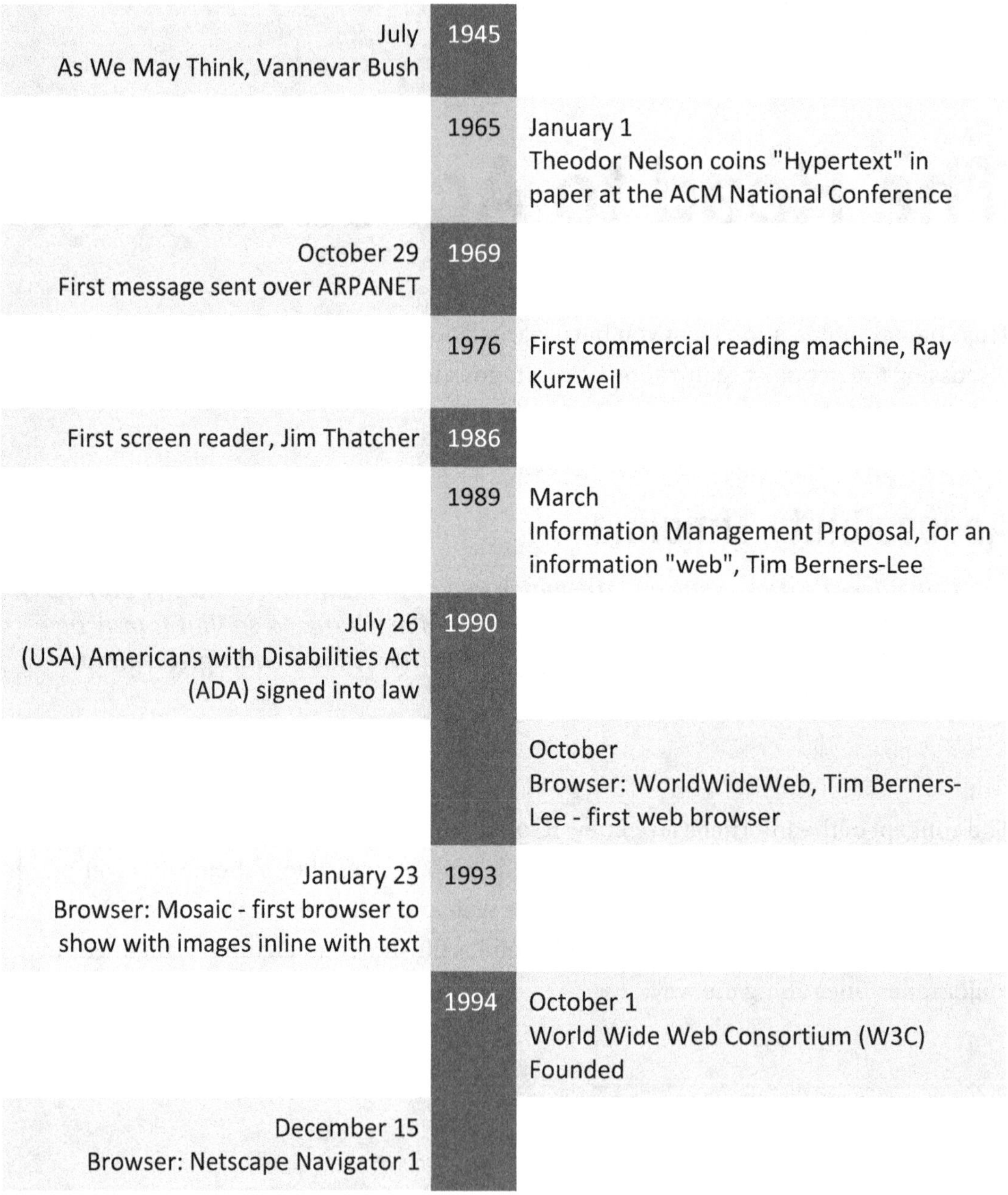

July As We May Think, Vannevar Bush	**1945**	
	1965	January 1 Theodor Nelson coins "Hypertext" in paper at the ACM National Conference
October 29 First message sent over ARPANET	**1969**	
	1976	First commercial reading machine, Ray Kurzweil
First screen reader, Jim Thatcher	**1986**	
	1989	March Information Management Proposal, for an information "web", Tim Berners-Lee
July 26 (USA) Americans with Disabilities Act (ADA) signed into law	**1990**	
		October Browser: WorldWideWeb, Tim Berners- Lee - first web browser
January 23 Browser: Mosaic - first browser to show with images inline with text	**1993**	
	1994	October 1 World Wide Web Consortium (W3C) Founded
December 15 Browser: Netscape Navigator 1		

Figure 2-1. *Major milestones of web accessibility*

	1995	(UK) Disability Discrimination Act 1995 passed by parliament
April 10 Browser: Opera 1		
		August 16 Browser: Internet Explorer 1.0
April 7 Web Accessibility Initiative (WAI) Official Launch	1997	
	1999	May 5 Web Content Accessibility Guidelines (WCAG) 1.0 Recommendation
December 21 (USA) Access Board issues final Accessibility Standards for Section 508 of the Rehabilitation Act of 1973	2000	
	2003	January 7 Browser: Safari 1
November 9 Browser: Firefox 1.0	2004	
	2006	September 26 WAI-ARIA First Public Draft
October 31 Convention on the Rights of Persons with Disabilities adopted by the UN		

Figure 2-1. *(continued)*

Figure 2-1. *(continued)*

World Wide Web (WWW)

In October of 1990 Tim Berners-Lee started work on the very first browser and coined the term "Word Wide Web," after which the browser was named (Figure 2-2). The browser was later renamed Nexus in order to prevent confusion between the browser and the concept.[2]

---

[2]Tim Berners-Lee, The WorldWideWeb browser, www.w3.org/People/Berners-Lee/WorldWideWeb.html, accessed December 8, 2018.

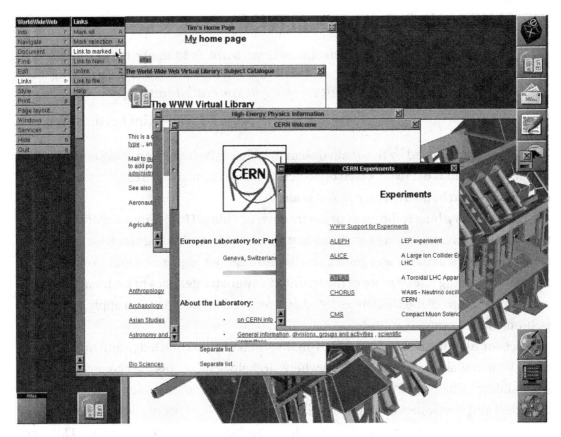

Figure 2-2. *Screenshot of the first browser[3]*

Shortly after, on August 6, 1991, the first web page went live at `http://info.cern.ch/hypertext/WWW/TheProject.html`.[4] With continued development, the need for standards became apparent. Urged by companies and firms who were investing more and more resources into the Web, on October 19, 1994, MIT announced the creation of the World Wide Web Consortium (W3C) founded by Tim Berners-Lee on October 1 at MIT in collaboration with CERN and with support from DARPA and the European Commission.

---

[3]`www.w3.org/History/1994/WWW/Journals/CACM/screensnap2_24c.gif`.

[4]Alyson Shontell, "FlashBack: This Is What the First-Ever Website Looked Like," *Business Insider*, `www.businessinsider.com/flashback-this-is-what-the-first-website-ever-looked-like-2011-6`, accessed December 8, 2018.

World Wide Web Consortium (W3C)

The essential work of the Web consortium team is to draw these threads together into a consistent architecture ensuring that the rapid pace of progress can be maintained without creeping incompatibilities.[5]

—Tim Berners-Lee

The W3C work is guided by two main design principles; Web on Everything and Web for All. The vision is to create a Web on which users can be active participants, share information, and build trust on a global scale.

Web on Everything is the basis of the Internet of Things (IoT). From smartphones to televisions to vehicles, we are increasingly surrounded by technology for which the W3C aims to provide standards and guidelines. Interestingly enough, since many of these devices are lacking one or more of the traditional human interfaces of keyboard, mouse, and display, many of the challenges faced by users with disabilities also apply to users of web-enabled devices.

Web for All is the basis of web accessibility – making the knowledge and opportunity of the Web available to everyone, everywhere. To help achieve this they created the Web Accessibility Initiative (WAI) which develops strategies, standards, and resources for designers and developers to help make the Web accessible to people with disabilities. While the W3C develops the general technical standards for the Web, such as HTML and CSS, WAI focuses specifically on accessibility.

Web Accessibility Initiative (WAI)

Web accessibility became an official project of the W3C as early as Fall of 1996. Early on, the accessibility information mainly consisted of a few pages regarding web accessibility for people with disabilities maintained by Mike Paciello and the Yuri Rubinski Insight Foundation. After securing support and funding, the official launch of the Web Accessibility Initiative (WAI) was held in Santa Clara in April of 1997.[6] Today WAI is responsible for creating the web accessibility guidelines which design and development teams follow to make their applications accessible to all.

---

[5]"LCS Announces Web Industry Consortium," *MIT News on campus and around the world,* `http://news.mit.edu/1994/lcs-1019`, accessed December 8, 2018.

[6]"WAI Early Days," *W3C Web Accessibility Initiative,* `www.w3.org/WAI/history`, accessed December 8, 2018.

Web Accessibility Guidelines

Content is accessed in different ways depending on its intended use. Users of web sites use tools such as browsers, assistive technologies, or media players to access content, and how this content is displayed depends on the user agent (device) used.

Authors of web sites who wish to edit their content use tools such as authoring tools or evaluation tools, which have their own guidelines. Figure 2-3 illustrates which guidelines are used for each type of content and by whom.

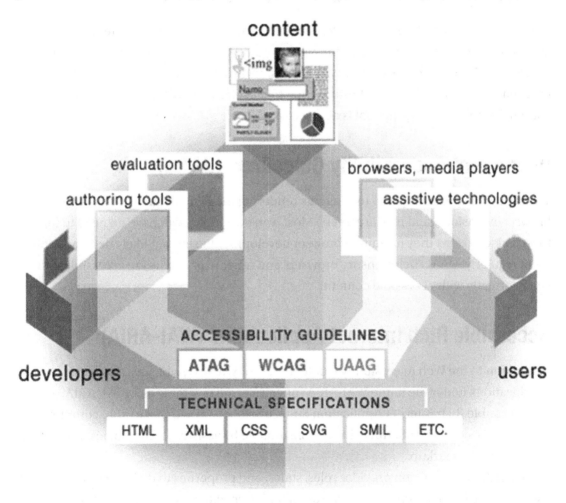

Figure 2-3. *Guidelines for the different components*[7]

---

[7]www.w3.org/WAI/content-images/wai-std-gl-overview/specs.png.

Web Content Accessibility Guidelines (WCAG)

The WCAG guidelines cover both display of content (such as images, text, code and markup, or sound) and user interaction, and are applicable to all web sites and web applications. These guidelines will be the focus of this book and are explored in greater detail in the next section.

Authoring Tool Accessibility Guidelines (ATAG)

The ATAG guidelines apply to tools content developers use to author content such as HTML editor, content management systems (CMS), and web sites that allow users to create their own content such as wikis, blogs, and social networking sites. ATAG guidelines not only help make the authoring tool itself accessible, but help ensure the content being created by the tool is also accessible.

User Agent Accessibility Guidelines (UAAG)

The UAAG guidelines apply to user agents rendering the content such as browsers, browser extensions, and media players. Most web developers will have no need to follow these guidelines, as they pertain to browser development itself, but likely depend upon them regularly. UAAG helps ensure browsers and other user agents are accessible and work correctly with accessible content.

Accessible Rich Internet Applications (WAI-ARIA)

In addition to the Web Accessibility Guidelines, the WAI also publishes technical specifications under the name WAI-ARIA (often referred to simply as ARIA). ARIA, the Accessible Rich Internet Application Suite, provides ways to make more complex components – often JavaScript driven – consumable by assistive technologies by labeling elements in the markup.

The ARIA specification provides roles, states, and properties to define accessible user interface (UI) elements as well as API mapping specifications and modules for graphics and digital publishing. These are used to express structures, behaviors, and state to assistive technologies. It is especially helpful with dynamic content and complex

UI controls developed using Web APIs, HTML, JavaScript, and related technologies. Essentially it creates a bridge between the host technology and dynamic content features.[8]

In large part ARIA helps developers describe *intent* in a manner that overlaps with existing web semantics. The use of this specification directly impacts both of the W3C's principles of Web for All and Web on Everything.

WCAG 2.1

WCAG 2.0, published in December of 2008, consisted of 12 guidelines, which provide testable success criteria within three levels of conformance.

Ten years later, in June of 2018 the WCAG 2.1 were published. The WCAG 2.1 recommendation includes WCAG 2.0 but adds a 13th guideline for Input Modalities to cover various input mechanisms (including touch). The updated recommendation also included 17 new success criteria which were added to existing guidelines. Even though a guideline was added, and some were extended, version 2.1 is fully backward compatible with 2.0. This means that conformance with WCAG 2.1 implies conformance with WCAG 2.0 as well.

Principles of Accessibility

Each guideline in the recommendation, with their associated success criteria, is organized around the following four foundational principles[9] that all web content must be Perceivable, Operable, Understandable, and Robust.

Under each of these principles are guidelines that describe specifically what needs to be achieved to conform including specific testable criteria.

Perceivable

Information and user interface components must be presentable to users in ways they can perceive.

All users must be able to discern the content being presented to them. This means that content cannot be hidden from users regardless of the technology they are using to access it.

---

[8]W3C's Accessible Rich Internet Applications (WAI-ARIA) 1.0 Expands Accessibility of the Open Web Platform, *W3C*, www.w3.org/2014/03/aria.html.en, accessed December 12, 2018.

[9]www.w3.org/TR/UNDERSTANDING-WCAG20/intro.html#introduction-fourprincs-head.

Operable

> *User interface components and navigation must be operable.*

All users can navigate and interact with the web page. The interface cannot be built in such a way that requires a user to perform an action they are incapable of performing.

Understandable

> *Information and the operation of user interface must be understandable.*

Users can understand the content being presented and how to interact with it. This involves two types of understanding. The content itself; the reading level used, content organization, etc., must be clear. And the interactions available on the page; users must be able to understand how to perform actions being required of them to use the application.

Robust

> *Content must be robust enough that it can be interpreted reliably by a wide variety of user agents, including assistive technologies.*

Dependence upon one specific user agent, browser, or assistive technology should be minimized as much as possible. Attention to existing web standards and guidelines should be maximized. In general, a user should be able to select the technology that works best for them and expect a reasonably consistent experience. The expectation is also that content must remain accessible, even as technologies and tools continue to change and evolve.

This also means that the same content, features, and interactions should be available across technologies. For example, actions capable of being performed on desktop should also be available on mobile.

Conformance

In general, conformance to a standard means that the requirements of the standard are met. The levels of conformance (Figure 2-4) address part of the challenge and variability inherent in the success criteria, but there is also a subjective aspect revolving around usability. The person performing your audit, or doing your testing, will greatly influence your specific implementation and results. Please keep in mind that just like holding a driver's license does not make you a safe driver, conformance to an accessibility standard does not imply that the content is accessible. However, conformance does provide a very useful framework for tracking progress and reporting issues that may arise.

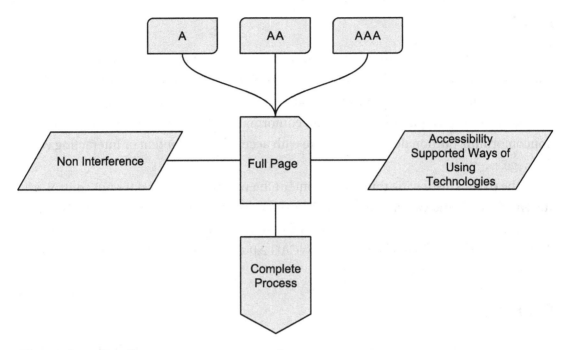

Figure 2-4. *Conformance*

Conformance Level

In an ideal world all applications would be perfectly accessible to all people, all the time regardless of technology. However, since we do not live in a perfect world, WCAG 2.0 and 2.1 have the following three levels of success criteria:

- **Level A**: The minimum level of conformance to meet WCAG. This is the lowest level of conformance.

- **Level AA**: To comply with AA, conformance to A and AA success criteria must be reached.

- **Level AAA**: For AAA conformance, level A, AA, and AAA success criteria must be met. This is the highest level conformance and most difficult to achieve.

It is worth noting that for some content AAA level cannot always be met and therefore requiring AAA level conformance as a general policy for an entire site is not recommended.

Full Pages

To meet conformance requires that the entire page's content at a minimum meets A level. Conformance cannot be achieved if part of the web page is excluded. If the page has content that is rendered accessible via an alternate version, the alternate version is considered part of the page and conformance can be reached as long as the nonconforming portion does not interfere with accessing the content or interacting with the page.

If the page is displaying third party content the web page author does not control, a **statement of partial conformance** can be used if the areas that are nonconforming are clearly defined. An example of a partial conformance statement would be "This page does not conform but would conform to WCAG 2.0 at level AA if the following parts from uncontrolled sources were removed."

Complete Process

When a web page is part of a process, all web pages in the process must be conformant. A common type of process is a multipage form or wizard but can be anything that requires a sequence of steps to accomplish a task. A page that is part of a process cannot be considered conformant unless the entire process is. Additionally, the Full Pages requirement applies to every page in the process, subject to partial conformance if applicable.

Accessibility-Supported Technologies

The application must use technologies users have access to and understand. The application only relies on ways of using technologies that are accessibility supported to meet acceptance criteria. **Accessibility supported** technologies require that the way in which the technology is being used needs to be supported by users' assistive technologies and that one of the following occurs:

- The technology is widely supported by user agents, such as CSS and HTML.

- The technology is supported in a widely supported plug-in.

- The content is on a closed environment where the technology required by the user agent is also used.

- The user agents that support the technology are as easily findable and purchasable for people with disabilities as to those without.

Noninterference

As much as nonconforming technologies can be used, or conforming technologies can be used in unsupported ways, they cannot interfere with using the application or accessing the content and the information still needs to be accessible using accessible methods.

Furthermore, the page must, if applicable, have audio controls (if applicable), be free of keyboard traps, keep any flashing under three flashes per second, and be able to pause, stop, or hide content that moves, blinks, scrolls, or auto-updates.

Conforming Alternate Version

For any level, if conformance cannot be met, an alternate version can be provided.

Alternate versions are a way to allow users to access content that cannot be otherwise made to conform. In order to be a "conforming alternate version" the alternate version must

1. Conform at the designated level

2. Provide all of the same information and functionality in the same human language

3. Be as up to date as the nonconforming content

4. Ensure at least one of the following is true:

    a. The conforming version can be reached from the nonconforming page via an accessibility-supported mechanism.

    b. The nonconforming version can only be reached from the conforming version.

    c. The nonconforming version can only be reached from a conforming page that also provides a mechanism to reach the conforming version.[10]

---

[10]Conforming Alternate Version, Web Content Accessibility Guidelines (WCAG) 2.0, www.w3.org/TR/UNDERSTANDING-WCAG20/conformance.html, accessed December 10, 2018.

Alternate versions are best used sparingly, as they do not provide the best possible experience for any of the users of your web site or application. These are an allowance provided by WCAG that acknowledges that incremental improvements are worth taking, and complete conformance is not always possible – especially for legacy systems.

It's important to remember that the goal of any accessibility initiative should be full access to all, rather than conformance to WCAG. The guidelines exist to provide standards by which accessibility can be measured objectively.

Success Criteria

Success criteria are written to have testable specifications that can involve human testing, automated testing, or both. Because conformance to the criteria doesn't guarantee that content is accessible by users with a wide variety of disabilities, usability testing is therefore also strongly recommended.

Conformance to WCAG is assessed based upon the individual success criteria, so an exploration of these criteria is at the heart of any web accessibility effort. The W3C has a convenient Quick Reference which provides an overview of the Principles, Guidelines, and Success Criteria of WCAG 2.1, available at `www.w3.org/WAI/WCAG21/quickref/`.

Reading the Spec

The WCAG documentation (Figure 2-5) organizes the guidelines by principle. Each guideline is then followed with what level of conformance the guideline is for, links to supporting documentation, and then the criterion that must be met in order to conform.

The full version of the WCAG guidelines can be found at `www.w3.org/TR/WCAG/`.

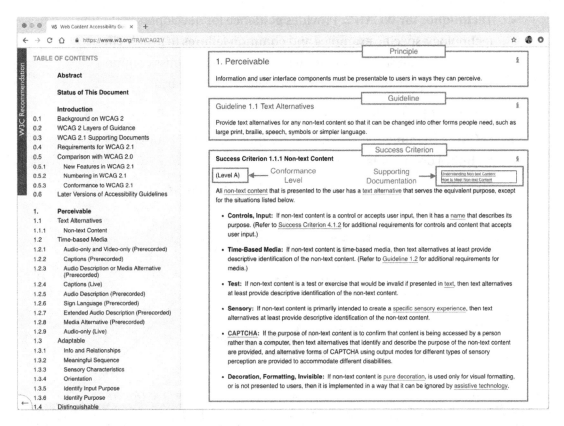

Figure 2-5. *Screenshot of WCAG 2.1*

The specification includes four types of supporting documents (Figure 2-6):

- **How to Meet WCAG 2:** A quick reference and checklist which includes all of the guidelines and their criteria.

  www.w3.org/WAI/WCAG21/quickref/

- **Understanding WCAG:** Gives extra information on the guidelines and the criteria. Talks to the intent of the guidelines and success criterion, how it helps people with disabilities, technology support notes, examples, and links to outside resources such as testing tools.

  www.w3.org/TR/UNDERSTANDING-WCAG/

- **Techniques for WCAG 2:** Provides guidance for developers including technology-specific examples and common failures to avoid. The failures warrant special attention as they tend to address common pitfalls and provide very specific indicators and scenarios.

  www.w3.org/TR/WCAG-TECHS/

- **WCAG 2 Documents:** Diagram, descriptions, and link for WCAG technical documents.

  www.w3.org/WAI/standards-guidelines/wcag/docs/

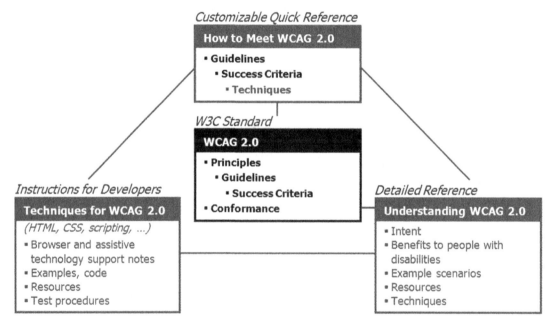

Figure 2-6. *Documentation types and their purposes*[11]

Key Contributors

Everyone has something to contribute to the World Wide Web. Why? Because the Web is of us. Whatever we are as humans is now manifest in the Web: Our beauty, hatred, fragility, and ferocity; our kindness, cruelty, confusion, and clarity. Our wars. Our peace.[12]

—Molly Holzschlag

---

[11]www.w3.org/WAI/content-images/wai-intro-wcag/wcag20docs.png.

[12]www.computerhope.com/people/molly_holzschlag.htm.

Universal accessibility of information has been a global effort undertaken by thousands of individuals over more than 70 years. Hopefully you and your teams will soon be joining this effort by establishing an action plan to achieve and maintain conformance with accessibility standards.

However, there are a few key individuals that have demonstrated tremendous vision and leadership in guiding us to an accessible Web of content and interactions.

Dr Vinton Cerf

Often referred to as the "Father of the Internet," Dr Vinton "Vint" Cerf[13] created some of the fundamental technologies of the Internet, along with coinventor Robert Kahn. Both Cerf and Kahn were honored with the Alan Mathison Turing Award for their "pioneering work on internetworking, including the design and implementation of the Internet's basic communications protocols, TCP/IP, and for inspired leadership in networking."[14]

While his early contributions laid the groundwork for the Internet, and the World Wide Web to follow, Cerf's later contributions have been as an advocate for accessibility and using Internet technology for the good of people around the world.

In a 2017 interview with CNET, Cerf had this to say about the state of Accessibility in the industry: "It can't be a pixie dust that you sprinkle on top of the program and suddenly make it accessible, which is the behavior pattern in the past. Accessibility should be a design choice that is rewarded, something a lot of companies have not stepped up to."[15]

This is something that is personal for Cerf, who has a hearing disability. Since its invention he has leaned heavily on e-mail for clear, precise communication because verbal communication is challenging for him. His wife, Sigrid Cerf, also has a hearing disability, becoming deaf at the age of 3 due to spinal meningitis. In a remarkable turn of fate, in 1995 Sigrid was able to use the Web to research cochlear implants, using e-mail to contact other implant recipients. After attempts to reach Johns Hopkins University failed via phone, Sigrid sent an e-mail directly to the doctor performing the operations, and received a reply the next day. She had the surgery in April 1996, and the next month she

---

[13]https://internethalloffame.org/inductees/vint-cerf.
[14]www.britannica.com/biography/Vinton-Cerf.
[15]www.cnet.com/news/internet-inventor-vint-cerf-accessibility-disability-deaf-hearing/.

was able to speak to Vint on the phone for the very first time,[16] as a result of the Internet technologies he had helped to create.

Raymond Kurzweil

Many people know Raymond "Ray" Kurzweil[17] as the futurist who has predicted the Singularity – an age of intelligent machines. Even more know of his work on electronic musical instruments.

But Kurzweil's first major project was a reading machine for the blind, capable of scanning text and turning it into speech. This creation required a number of other inventions including the CCD flatbed scanner, any-font Optical Character Recognition (OCR), and speech synthesizer.

The company behind this innovation, Kurzweil Computer Products, announced the Kurzweil Reading Machine in 1976. The announcement attracted quite a lot of attention, resulting in a live demo of the machine on the Today Show. The demo caught the attention of Stevie Wonder, a legendary musician well known for being blind. This led to the first production version of the reading machine being quickly assembled for the musician.[18]

In 1980, Kurzweil Computer Products was sold to Xerox, providing a key component to that company's document technology. While Xerox was primarily interested in the optical innovations, the work on speech synthesis led to innovations in musical instruments. In 1982, Kurzweil Music Systems was founded, in collaboration with Stevie Wonder.

In a 2004 interview with the American Foundation for the Blind,[19] Kurzweil discusses the advances in technology – specifically mobile devices – that have made it possible to develop reading machines primarily as software, usable on consumer products. He also notes, "Blind people work in every area. Of course, it's not just technology. It requires education, training, it requires society to cooperate in terms of overcoming ancient prejudices. But the technology plays an important role, in terms of being able to provide alternative ways of doing the same thing."

From his years of work in technology and accessibility, Kurzweil has received many recognitions for his technology innovations including 20 honorary doctorates,

---

[16]www.littlemag.com/listen/vintoncerf.html/ https://archive.nytimes.com/www.nytimes.com/library/cyber/week/021398deaf.html.

[17]www.kurzweiltech.com/aboutray.html.

[18]www.kurzweiltech.com/kcp.html.

[19]www.afb.org/info/living-with-vision-loss/using-technology/interviews-with-technology-pioneers/ray-kurzweil/part-1-of-4/12345.

a Technical Grammy Award, the MIT Lemelson Prize, and the US National Medal of Technology. In 2002 he was inducted into the National Inventors Hall of Fame.[20]

Dr Jim Thatcher

Before spending 37 years at IBM, Dr Jim Thatcher became one of the very first PhD recipients in Computer Science, in 1963. He joined IBM around the same time as his former thesis adviser from the University of Michigan, Dr Jesse Wright.[21]

The computer terminals of the time were completely inaccessible to Wright, who was blind. During the development of the personal computer (PC), they saw an opportunity and began working together on a new audio access system. This work culminated in the creation of one of the first screen readers for DOS in 1984, called the IBM Screen Reader, which became the namesake for such systems. Thatcher later expanded this product into the very first screen reader with a graphical user interface, available on the PC.

Thatcher continued working in accessibility throughout his career, joining the IBM Accessibility Center in 1996 and helping establish the IBM Accessibility Guidelines for IBM's development community. These guidelines in turn influenced the WAI. He co-authored *Constructing Accessible Web Sites*, which was published in the United States by Apress in July 2003.[22]

Thatcher has received numerous awards for his contributions, including the Distinguished Service award from The National Federation of the Blind, Vice President's Hammer Award, and the Association for Computing Machinery (ACM) lifetime achievement award from the Special Interest Group on Accessible Computing.

Janina Sajka

Ms Janina Sajka is a concert pianist and composer of electronic music, completing her Bachelor of Arts in Music in 1970. She has recorded and performed in a wide range of styles, receiving musical training from four different universities. Her career began focusing more on computer technology through the 1980s as she began experiencing diminished vision, reducing her access to printed information.[23]

---

[20]www.kurzweilai.net/ray-kurzweil-biography.

[21]www.sigaccess.org/2008/04/jim-thatcher-outstanding-contribution-recipient-2008/.

[22]www.afb.org/afbpress/pubnew.asp?DocID=aw050207.

[23]https://rednote.net/shortbio.txt.

By the 1990s Sajka was fully invested in the field of accessible technology, including technology policy. She worked at the World Institute on Disability, and later at the American Foundation for the Blind (AFB), where she participated in the design of accessible workstation and network environments. From 1999 to 2004 Sajka was Director of Technology Research at AFB where she became heavily involved in technology standards and processes, including the US Section 508 accessibility standards.

Over the years Sajka has served in many accessibility groups, including Special Working Group on Accessibility in the ISO/IEC Joint Technical Committee 1 (JTC 1) and the Linux Foundation Accessibility Workgroup (now the Open Accessibility Group) as Executive Chair. For the W3C she served as Chair of the WAI Independent User Interface Working Group and also the Chair of the WAI Protocols and Formats Working Group which was responsible for creating the WAI-ARIA.[24]

Sir Tim Berners-Lee

In 1989, while working at CERN, Sir Tim Berners-Lee invented the World Wide Web as a platform for information management, geared at global sharing and discoverability of information. The following year he completed the first web browser and the first web server. In so doing he initiated several critical technical specifications for interoperability, including URIs, HTTP, and HTML.[25]

Berners-Lee founded the W3C in 1994 as a global community responsible for developing and publishing web standards and recommendations. In September 1996 he wrote the following for the member newsletter: "The emergence of the World Wide Web has made it possible for individuals with appropriate computer and telecommunications equipment to interact as never before. It presents new challenges and new hopes to people with disabilities."[26]

As the figurehead for web technology and web accessibility, Berners-Lee remains an ongoing advocate for both. For his contributions he has been awarded the Millennium Prize and Alan Mathison Turing Award, and he is an inductee of the Internet Hall of Fame.

---

[24]https://tap.gallaudet.edu/Emergency/Nov05Conference/Emergency-Bios.html.
[25]https://internethalloffame.org/inductees/tim-berners-lee.
[26]www.w3.org/WAI/history.

Molly Holzschlag

While the Web was being conceived at CERN, Molly Holzschlag was launching her career in Internet technology. She published her first book on web design in 1996, going on to write more than 35 books on web technology and design. She has been widely recognized as one of the most influential women on the Web. One of her long-time friends and colleagues once quipped, "If Tim Berners-Lee is the father of the Web, then Molly is its fairy godmother," a title which stuck.[27]

From the beginning she was an advocate for an open, accessible Web. In 2007 she famously confronted Bill Gates on the status of standards compliance related to the upcoming Internet Explorer version 8 (IE8).[28] From 2004 to 2006 she was a Group Lead for the Web Standards Project (WaSP), which was founded in 1998 to arbitrate the browser wars and advocate for the users and developers of the Web.

Holzschlag has worked directly with CERN, AOL, Microsoft, BBC, eBay, Opera, and Netscape to ensure browsers support modern standards. She has been Chair of the W3C CSS Accessibility Community Group and a W3C invited expert to both the Internationalization Guidelines, Education and Outreach Working Group, and the HTML Working Group.[29]

Mike Paciello

For more than 35 years Mike Paciello[30] has been working on usability and accessibility. When he was working at DEC in the 1980s, computer interaction was largely text based, and technical guides were printed. He volunteered as a liaison with the National Braille Press on a project to convert documentation into braille, which was a heavily manual process at the time. During this time, he helped develop electronic documentation (and associated standards) that could be magnified on the screen, read by screen readers, and output to braille.

Few individuals have been more influential than Paciello in establishing accessibility standards for documentation, web content, and software. Starting in 1995 Paciello

---

[27]http://thewebahead.net/guest/molly-holzschlag.

[28]http://web.archive.org/web/20110113144025/ www.molly.com/2007/12/05/ conversation-with-bill-gates-about-ie8-and-microsoft-transparency/.

[29]www.computerhope.com/people/molly_holzschlag.htm.

[30]www.accessibilityonline.org/ada-tech/speakers/10072/.

began working on the creation of the WAI, until its successful launch 2 years later. He was an author of the first version of the WCAG and helped develop the 2001 Section 508 technology standards, and co-led the 2008 rewrite of Section 508/Section 255 standards.[31]

Wendy Chisholm

Wendy Chisholm was introduced into the world of accessibility during her undergraduate work in Computer Science. She tutored a blind student, developing tactile teaching tools along the way. She also coached a Special Olympics team as part of an after-school program for people with autism. When she went on to graduate school, she studied Human Factors, earning a Master of Science in Industrial Engineering.[32]

After graduating, Chisholm started working in the W3C Recommendation process as an editor on WCAG 1.0. She continued with the W3C for 7 more years as an editor on WCAG 2.0. After leaving the W3C she began consulting, providing assessment, education, and development services for clients including Microsoft, Google, Adobe, and the American Foundation for the Blind. During this time, she assisted University of Washington with the development of the browser-based WebAnywhere screen reader.

Today Chisholm is a Principal Accessibility Architect at Microsoft where she works on the Artificial Intelligence for Accessibility Program, with the goal of developing better solutions to support more than 1 billion people worldwide with a disability.[33]

Dr Cyndi Rowland

For most of her career Dr Cyndi Rowland has been the executive director of Web Accessibility in Mind (WebAIM), the nonprofit organization she founded in 1999. WebAIM is based at Utah State University, where Rowland earned her PhD in Special Education. She is also the Technology Director for the National Center on Disability and Access to Education (NCDAE) which is also based at Utah State University.[34]

---

[31]https://rosenfeldmedia.com/a-web-for-everyone/accessibility-standards-an-interview-with-mike-paciello/.

[32]www.w3.org/People/wendy/.

[33]http://sp1ral.com/about/.

[34]https://onlinelearningconsortium.org/person/cyndi-rowland-founder-executive-director-webaim/.

Through her organizations Rowland supports research, tool development, and education along with policy and standards development. She was a member of the Access Board's advisory committee for the Section 508 refresh and has engaged with the UN to guide development of global guidelines for accessible online distance education.[35]

Summary

In this chapter you have learned about the history of the World Wide Web, including the people involved in its development and advocating for accessibility. Specifically, you now know about:

- The W3C and its mission to maintain web standards and promote accessibility

- The WAI and its web accessibility guidelines

- Web Content Accessibility Guidelines (WCAG) and the A, AA, and AAA levels of conformance

- Four principles of accessible web content, that is, Perceivable, Operable, Understandable, and Robust

Web accessibility has taken many people with a variety of skills. The next chapter will help you understand what roles other people will play in your own accessibility projects and discuss how to get them involved.

---

[35]www.nten.org/ntc/speakers/cyndi-rowland/.

CHAPTER 3

Getting Your Team on Board

This chapter looks at the role of your team or company in a web accessibility initiative and discusses how to get them engaged and trained on their new responsibilities.

Involving the Team

Like many things, the best time to start considering accessibility is from the beginning. It is always better to integrate accessibility into the workflow from the beginning rather than retrofitting at the end. This will produce a better end result with less impact to your product timeline. By incorporating accessibility while designing the application, usability is greatly improved and as a bonus will provide the practice your team needs to become really familiar with accessibility concerns.

Whether you are starting a brand new project or making an existing project accessible, getting the entire team and stakeholders involved and on board is important to the success of any accessibility initiative.

Motivation

When you incent, people optimize for reward. When you inspire, people optimize for purpose.

—Michael Norton[1]

---

[1]"WebAIM's Hierarchy for Motivating Accessibility Change," WebAIM, https://webaim.org/blog/motivating-accessibility-change/, accessed January 13, 2019.

M. Dowden and M. Dowden, *Approachable Accessibility*, https://doi.org/10.1007/978-1-4842-4881-2_3

Depending on their role on the team or in the organization, each individual may be motivated by different factors to accept accessibility as part of the requirement and process for a project. These can be ethical, legal, economic, or personal.

Ethical: Accessibility is the right thing to do because it helps provide all users equal access to information and services. Individuals choosing to support an accessibility initiative because it is the right thing to do will generally yield the best results.

Legal: Several countries have laws regarding accessibility standards. Depending on the project and situation, it may be legally required for the project to meet certain accessibility standards and failing to meet that requirement may result in legal action being taken against the company. Examples include Australia's "Disability Discrimination Act 1992," the United Kingdom's "Equality Act 2010," and the United State's "Section 508 of the US Rehabilitation Act of 1973."[2]

Economic: Lost market share and revenue due to users' lack of ability to use the application and competitive advantages gained for being accessible. In the United States there are 49 million Americans with disability who control an estimated $175 billion in discretionary income. For many businesses, skipping accessibility is potentially excluding 20% of their total market.[3]

Personal: Whether they are personally affected by accessibility in some way, or perhaps have friends or family members that experience handicap, they have a personal motive driving them to support accessibility initiatives. They tend to understand the importance and the impact it can have on others. In the United States it is estimated that 30% of all families have at least one disabled member.

Short of personal motivation, many people are simply not informed enough to be swayed by ethical, legal, or economic reasons. One of your most important tasks in getting a team committed to accessibility is to educate them about these factors and find the one that will motivate them to get more involved.

It is important to use positive motivators such as encouragement and rewards rather than negative motivators such as guilt or punishment.

---

[2]www.w3.org/WAI/policies/?q=wcag-20.

[3]"Training Others: Why Accessibility? Motivating Learners to Bring About Change," WebAIM, https://webaim.org/articles/training/motivate, accessed January 4, 2019.

Team Roles

It is easy to say that adding accessibility to your products is the responsibility of the developers, but developers cannot do it alone. Outside factors such as designs being provided having inaccessible colors, time allotted to complete tasks being too short to deliver accessible features, and accessibility not being tested for, may even render the task impossible. Getting everyone involved and on the same page removes these barriers. Even though accessibility is the responsibility of the entire team, each role brings a different set of concerns.[4,5,6]

Business Leadership

Leadership is responsible for supporting accessibility efforts and making sure that accessibility is a business goal. This includes budgeting for training and software to allow the teams to meet their accessibility objective.

Managers, product owners, and project managers are responsible for determining the accessibility level projects must meet--and therefore standards to follow--and for making sure that time is allotted to accessibility development, testing, and resolving of any issues found.

Business stakeholders are in a great position to advocate for accessibility as they often are the decision makers in timelines, requirements, and budgets but also have the opportunity to lead by example.

Marketing/Branding/Design

As they are responsible for dictating brand colors, typefaces, and language used, it is imperative that those standards be accessible. Often the brand team will produce a style guide to allow for consistency across company communications and artifacts. These standards should be reviewed for accessibility so that "staying on brand" does not negatively affect accessibility.

---

[4]"Building a Culture of Accessibility: Leadership Roles," Deque, www.deque.com/blog/building-culture-accessibility-leadership-roles/, accessed January 5, 2019.

[5]"Accessibility and Empathy Creating the Best Digital Experience," Nerdery, www.nerdery.com/insights/accessibility-and-empathy-creating-the-best-digital-experience-for-disabled-users, accessed January 5, 2019.

[6]"Accessibility Is Everyone's Job: A Role-Based Model for Teams," simply accessible, https://simplyaccessible.com/article/role-based-a11y/, accessed January 5, 2019.

Web Designers

Designers generally concern themselves with user experience, look and feel, layout, interactions, content organization, and much more.

Understanding the accessibility standards that the application will adhere to is important in this role so that the web site can be designed to support them from the very beginning. Things to keep in mind as a designer are color contrasts, using more than just color to convey meaning, font sizes, alternate navigation options, and content organization. Collaborating with users, developers, and quality assurance (QA) when creating designs will help ensure that implementation ends up accessible.

If personas are being used as part of the design process, it is important to remember that even though they are archetypes for users, everyone is different and this includes people with disabilities. There are many types of disabilities with a wide variety of abilities, experiences, and preferences. Multiple personas will be necessary to cover the wide variety of interactions, and ongoing feedback from a diverse group of users is always preferable to constructed personas. When creating personas with disabilities, things to consider include

- Making sure the persona is not just a disability: Focus on abilities rather than the disability itself

- Nature of the limitations (blind, is in a noisy environment, easily distracted, etc.)

- Tools and strategies used (screen reader, keyboard user, trackball, etc.)

Content Creators

Content creators are often responsible for adding text, links, and images to sites. To maintain accessibility it's important that they ensure that the content and templates follow accessibility guidelines by minding heading structures, alternate text for images, reading level, and that link and button text is present and descriptive.

Content itself is often overlooked in accessibility testing. Including regular content review for accessibility will help ensure that the content itself stays accessible. Worth noting is that not all content management systems are capable of generating an accessible output, and therefore this needs to be considered during procurement.

Developers

They are the ones building the web sites and applications. They should be familiar with accessibility standards, ARIA, and semantic markup. Adding automated accessibility testing as part of unit and integration testing will help maintain component quality. They may need access to training in order to get familiarized with coding for accessibility.

Access to the technologies they need to support is important to test while developing and to understand how they work.

Testing/QA

Testers should include a combination of automated, manual, and usability testing. Automated testing can cover some basics including the presence of alternate text on images, but cannot assess whether the text was meaningful or descriptive. Manual testing fills that gap and should include a variety of devices and techniques such as screen readers, keyboard-only, screen magnifiers, etc. Usability testing allows actual users to determine if the application fulfills their needs. It is invaluable in catching issues that might be missed because of the intimate knowledge held by the business and development team about the application and its inner workings. More details about accessibility testing will be provided in the next chapter.

Legal/Compliance/HR

They are responsible for making sure everyone in the organization knows any policies the company may have toward accessibility as well as if there are any legal requirements attached to them and the consequences for nonconformance.

They may also be responsible for producing accessibility statements and conformance documentation. An accessibility statement provides information about the accessibility of the content and shows commitment to producing accessible content. These include a commitment to provide accessibility, inclusion of people with disabilities, specific standards and levels that are being followed, and contact information to report issues. They can also have extra information including supported technologies, measures taken to ensure accessibility, or known limitations.

Education

Education is the most powerful weapon which you can use to change the world.

—Nelson Mandela[7]

Statistics and descriptions such as those provided in Chapter 1 can provide an overview of what some of the disabilities are and how the user is affected, but education must go beyond numbers.

Education about disabilities, what they are, and their impact on the users allows the team to understand the obstacles they are trying to remove. This can involve learning more about specific disabilities and handicaps, and using assistive technology.

However, there are many other important topics related to web accessibility. Developers must understand the technical details of implementing WCAG and ARIA. Designers and testers need to be able to use assistive devices to ensure a good web experience.

Simulators

To get a glimpse into the experience that a disabled user might have while using an application, simulations can be used. Simulators can be used to imitate what it is like to have a certain handicap by altering the view in order to mimic the disadvantage. There are simulators available which can be used to understand what it is like to use a website or web application with cognitive disability, low-vision conditions, dyslexia, or motor impairment.

Cognition

Cognition handicap simulators will try to mimic a neuroatypical user's experience. Most attempt to simulate the effects of cognitive overload. They might jumble letters in order to simulate dyslexia, throw distracting pop-ups and sounds while you are attempting to look at the page to simulate ADD, or have you complete multiple tasks at the same time to show the effects of distractibility. The simulator shown in Figure 3-1 has the user complete a series of tasks while moving the stick figure around to prevent bombs from landing on it. The goal is to mimic distractibility and cognitive overload.

---

[7]"Nelson Mandela on the Power of Education," The Washington Post, www.washingtonpost.com/news/answer-sheet/wp/2013/12/05/nelson-mandelas-famous-quote-on-education/?utm_term=.269432e4b028, accessed January 4, 2019.

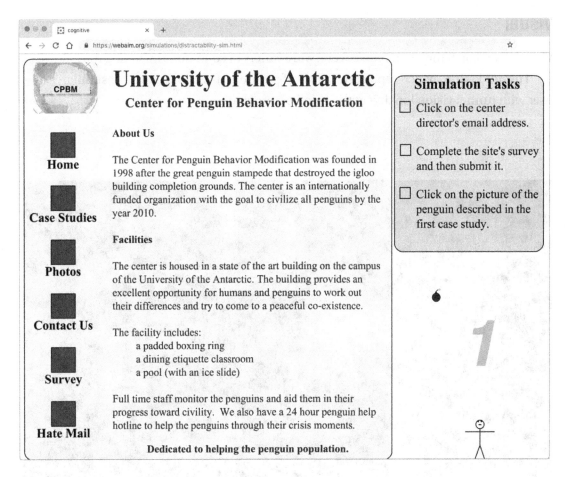

Figure 3-1. *Distractibility simulation[8]*

Motor Control

Motor Handicap Simulations include making the cursor tremble in order to replicate the tremors caused by Parkinson or removing the user's ability to use a mouse or trackpad in order to force the use of an alternate form of navigation. Asking team members to go without a mouse or trackpad for an afternoon can be a very revealing experience, exposing some of the struggles shared by users who cannot use a mouse.

---

[8]https://webaim.org/simulations/distractability-sim.html.

Visual

Visual Handicap Simulations can cover a wide variety of conditions including the following.

Tunnel Vision, which represents a loss of peripheral vision. Figure 3-2 simulates a user with tunnel vision looking at the Google homepage.

Figure 3-2. *Funkify Disability Simulator[9] with persona "Tunnel Toby" enabled*

---

[9]`www.funkify.org/`.

Central Scotoma, where the central field of vision is diminished, leaving primarily the peripheral vision. Figure 3-3 shows what a user with this condition might see.

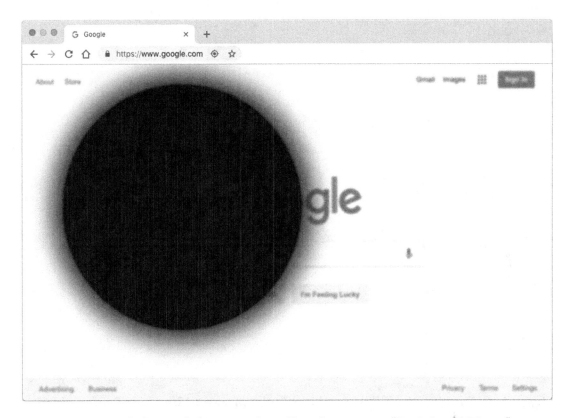

Figure 3-3. *Funkify Disability Simulator[10] with persona "Peripheral Pierre" enabled*

---

[10]www.funkify.org/.

Glare due to sunshine such as in Figure 3-4.

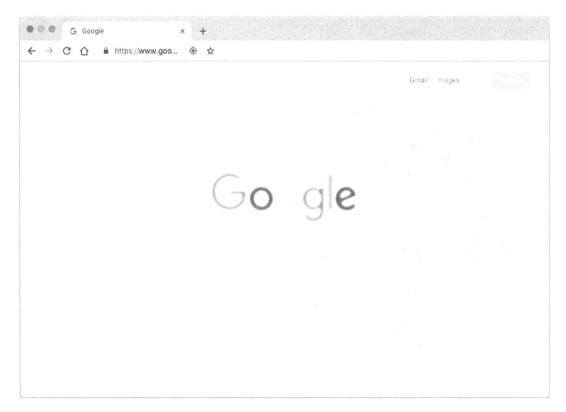

Figure 3-4. *Funkify Disability Simulator[11] with persona "Sunshine Sue" enabled*

---

[11]www.funkify.org/.

Blurred Vision. Figure 3-5 shows a simulation of Google's search autocomplete for a user with blurred vision.

Figure 3-5. *Funkify Disability Simulator[12] with persona "Blurry Bianca" enabled*

---

[12]www.funkify.org/.

Color Blindness. Figures 3-6 to 3-9 show the same web page for a user without color blindness vs. what users with different types of color blindness might see.

Figure 3-6. *Normal vision*

Figure 3-7. *Grayscale (achromatopsia)*

Figure 3-8. *Blue/yellow (tritanopia)*

Figure 3-9. *Red/green (protanopia)*

Also valuable when simulating loss of vision is experiencing what it is like to use a screen reader. Screen readers are interfaces that communicate content rendered on the screen via speech synthesizer or braille display. Interacting with a screen reader not only exposes a vastly different interaction than what abled users are used to but also provides insights into a tool developers will need to support.

Testing and Feedback

Simulations can be useful when trying to judge how accessible a button is (can it be clicked easily, is the target area large enough to do this, is its purpose of being a clickable button obvious), or whether color contrast needs to be adjusted. However, simulations are *not* a holistic view into what it is like to be a disabled user. They fail to account for coping mechanisms acquired and frustrations experienced by users who live with disability every day and should be used as an aid and not as a substitute for interacting with disabled individuals.[13]

The best way to understand how users are impaired by a web site's inner workings is by regularly interacting with your users and soliciting their feedback. Be sure to include users with a wide range of abilities when performing user testing and building focus groups. Include assistive technology alongside mobile devices and web browsers when performing usability and compatibility testing. Keep in mind that many users

---

[13]Nario-Redmond, M. R., Gospodinov, D., & Cobb, A. (2017, March 13), Crip for a Day: The Unintended Negative Consequences of Disability Simulations, Rehabilitation Psychology, Advance online publication, https://doi.org/10.1037/rep0000127.

of your web sites or web applications who experience either permanent or situational handicap likely do not think of themselves as disabled. They are simply aware that your application is hard for them to use.

One of the most important things to remember is to practice empathy. It is your responsibility to provide the best web experience you can across all ability levels, but nobody is obligated to explain what it is like to live with a disability.

Summary

In this chapter you have learned how to get your team involved in accessibility initiatives, across a variety of roles. Specifically, you now know

- Each team member may have a different motivational factor.

- It is important to use positive, inspirational motivators.

- Your team should get hands-on with simulators and assistive technology.

- Everyone has a role to play in successful web accessibility.

In the next chapter we will cover how to get started testing your application, highlighting areas requiring special attention.

CHAPTER 4

Getting Started

In this chapter we will cover how to get started testing an application for accessibility issues. This includes decisions that will need to be made, automated testing, and gaps where manual testing will be necessary.

Determining Scope

So you are ready to make your application accessible, which is awesome! But how much work is it going to be? The following sections will help you gauge how much work there is to be done.

Accessibility Acceptance Level

In an ideal world, all projects would strive for the highest level of accessibility possible; however, there are often extra factors that mean this is not always possible. The first thing to do is determine the appropriate level of conformance. Each project will vary based on several factors including which country the users are in and the users that the app serves. Notwithstanding, it's important to remember that reaching a higher level of accessibility than what the current demographic requires will open up the application to use by a currently unserved user base. Demographic research and guidance from your legal or compliance team at this juncture will help determine what an appropriate level of conformance is, and if there are any additional legal requirements that need to be fulfilled. We will focus on WCAG conformance only. See Chapter 2 for more details on the WCAG conformance levels A, AA, and AAA.

Once a level is chosen, a baseline assessment of the application can be done to determine what will need to be fixed and the amount of work it will involve. To determine what needs to be tested and how to best perform that testing, the supported browsers and assistive technologies will also need to be chosen.

© Martine Dowden and Michael Dowden 2019
M. Dowden and M. Dowden, *Approachable Accessibility*, https://doi.org/10.1007/978-1-4842-4881-2_4

Browser Support

Browsers have different rendering engines and intricacies as to how they implement the HTML, CSS, and JavaScript specifications, which may affect the available features. Because of this, the same code can have different behaviors depending on which browser it is rendered in.

As of December of 2018, the market was divided as shown in Figure 4-1.

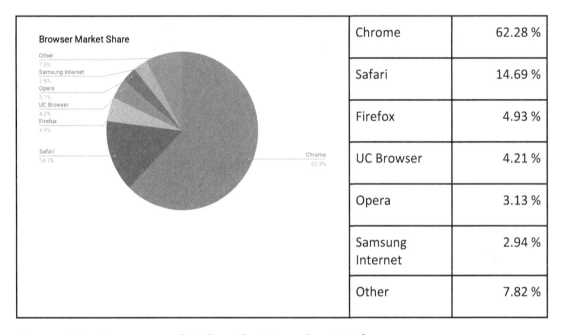

Chrome	62.28 %
Safari	14.69 %
Firefox	4.93 %
UC Browser	4.21 %
Opera	3.13 %
Samsung Internet	2.94 %
Other	7.82 %

Figure 4-1. *Browser market share for December 2018[1]*

When looking at device specific market share the stats change a little for desktop and mobile as shown in Figures 4-2 and 4-3.

---

[1]`http://gs.statcounter.com/browser-market-share`.

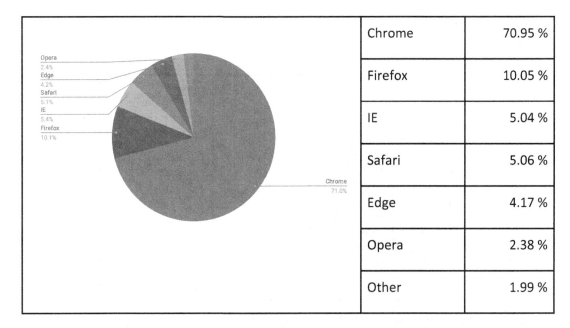

Chrome	70.95 %
Firefox	10.05 %
IE	5.04 %
Safari	5.06 %
Edge	4.17 %
Opera	2.38 %
Other	1.99 %

Figure 4-2. *Desktop browser market share for December 2018*[2]

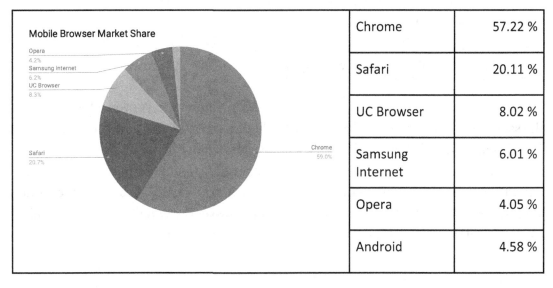

Chrome	57.22 %
Safari	20.11 %
UC Browser	8.02 %
Samsung Internet	6.01 %
Opera	4.05 %
Android	4.58 %

Figure 4-3. *Mobile market share for December 2018*[3]

---

[2]http://gs.statcounter.com/browser-market-share/desktop/worldwide.

[3]http://gs.statcounter.com/browser-market-share/mobile/worldwide.

With a device distribution showing a pretty even split between mobile and desktop. See Figure 4-4.

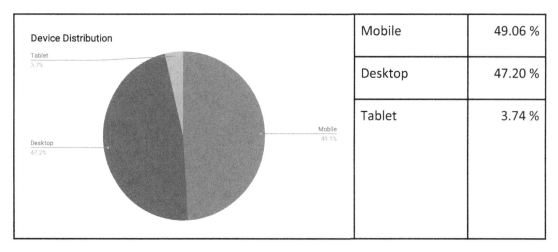

Mobile	49.06 %
Desktop	47.20 %
Tablet	3.74 %

Figure 4-4. Device distribution for December 2018[4]

Understanding the usage trends for the specific application can help guide decisions based on what they are using.

Assistive Technology Support

Just like browsers, assistive technologies may work in different ways even if they are the same type. For example, JAWS and NVDA, both screen readers, have their own implementation and often exhibit different behaviors when run on the same code.

Typically, a screen reader works in combination with a standard web browser, which can yield a large number of possible combinations. According to a WebAIM survey from October of 2017 the most common screen reader/browser combination was JAWS with Internet Explorer. Figure 4-5 shows a more detailed breakdown.

---

[4]http://gs.statcounter.com/platform-market-share/desktop-mobile-tablet.

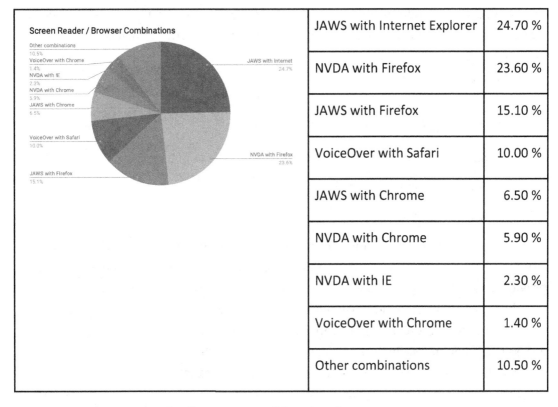

JAWS with Internet Explorer	24.70 %
NVDA with Firefox	23.60 %
JAWS with Firefox	15.10 %
VoiceOver with Safari	10.00 %
JAWS with Chrome	6.50 %
NVDA with Chrome	5.90 %
NVDA with IE	2.30 %
VoiceOver with Chrome	1.40 %
Other combinations	10.50 %

Figure 4-5. *Screen reader/browser combinations[5]*

Unlike browser and device versions and types, screen reader usage cannot just be detected via analytics. Even if we could, there are some serious privacy and ethics considerations regarding this kind of data as it could easily be used in order to discriminate against disabled users. User research is currently the best and most ethical way to understand what assistive technologies users are utilizing and how.

Accessibility Statement

Once the technologies that are going to be tested and supported have been chosen, along with an accessibility level, it is recommended that an accessibility statement be drafted and published.

---

[5]https://webaim.org/projects/screenreadersurvey7/.

An accessibility statement will not only show users that you care about them and that accessibility is a primary concern but also give users information about accessibility implementation on your app.

Things to include are

- A commitment to accessibility and inclusion of people with disabilities

- Specific accessibility standards applied

- Browsers and tools tested on and with

- Known limitations

And most importantly, include contact information so that should a user encounter issues, or have questions or comments about the application, they have an avenue to provide feedback and get answers.

The accessibility statement will need to be updated as accessibility improvements are made to the web site or application. More information about how to write accessibility statements, including a generator tool, can be found on the W3C Web Accessibility Initiative web site at `www.w3.org/WAI/planning/statements/`.

Initial Assessment

At this point it is tempting to start running accessibility checker tools on your web pages to see what is what, but there is more to be considered.

Regardless of whether you are conducting the initial assessment in-house or having an external agency perform an audit, understanding the application's front-end architecture will help you make sure that areas are not accidentally overlooked.

Flows and Processes

Procuring a site map for all pages and flow diagrams for processes will ensure that each activity can be tested and properly evaluated. Access roles are a factor in this as well if the site has content that is only displayed for certain types of users or only if certain conditions are met. Understanding how to get to each piece of content will make testing easier and more effective. Good product documentation will help tremendously in any accessibility initiative.

When enumerating the pages and processes to test, it's important to keep in mind that at least some of the assessment work will likely be performed by someone not familiar with the application. It is also important to identify areas of functionality that are only available based upon specific data being in place.

For the application to be considered conformant, key features and all pages comprising the steps for accomplishing the end goal of the feature must be conformant. Having a list of these features and their steps is paramount so that they all can be checked for accessibility issues. Taking an ecommerce site as an example, selecting products, adding them to a cart, reviewing the cart, and checking out, all need to be accessible for the site to be considered accessible. If any part is nonconforming, then the site does not meet conformance standards.

Third-Party Integrations

If the application uses third-party elements such as libraries, external components, or content management tools, research regarding their accessibility support, capabilities, and limitations will be necessary. If any of them cannot be made conformant and replacement is impossible, then alternate flows or partial conformance will need to be considered for those elements. Documentation from third-party tools can be a great source of guidance for how to achieve the necessary conformance. Many third-party integrations will provide implementation instructions for achieving accessibility while utilizing their product. For example, Angular Material does this through notes at the bottom of their component overview pages and in their Component Dev Kit (CDK) documentation (Figure 4-6).

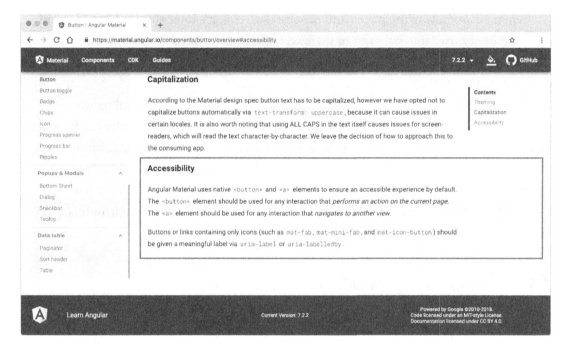

Figure 4-6. *Angular Material button component accessibility details[6]*

Breakpoints

Especially with the current mobile-first trend, many applications are now built in a responsive manner as it makes it easier to scale up content then to try and create a mobile view once the larger views have been created. A responsive web site is characterized by using web technologies such as HTML, CSS, and JavaScript to resize, hide, or rearrange content based on the size of the viewport (browser or device window) in which the content is being displayed. The goal is to make the site look good regardless of device or window size. To achieve this, breakover points are set at which display behavior changes. Figures 4-7 and 4-8 show the same web site when the window is 1024 pixels wide (Figure 4-7) vs. a viewport of 500 pixels wide (Figure 4-8).

---

[6]https://material.angular.io/components/button/overview#accessibility.

Figure 4-7. *Apress web site – Viewport size 1024 × 800 pixels*[7]

Figure 4-8. *Apress web site – Viewport size 500 × 800 pixels*

[7]www.apress.com/us.

One technique often used is CSS media queries. These allow the developers to target different viewport sizes and alter styles accordingly. In the application's Cascading Style Sheet (CSS) the code might look something like the following:

```
@media (min-width: 500px) {
    button {
        background: blue;
    }
}
```

In this CSS example, when the viewport size is greater than or equal to 500 pixels, buttons will have a blue background (Figures 4-9 and 4-10).

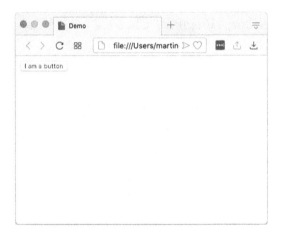

Figure 4-9. *Viewport less than 500px*

Figure 4-10. *Viewport more than 500px*

In this way, viewport height and width, screen resolution, and device orientation can be targeted. Because the UI changes based on the device and viewport size, there is a potential for accessibility issues to be found only when within certain viewport size ranges or screen resolutions. Imagine this scenario if the button text color is also blue – it would be invisible for some users, but only those using specific viewport sizes. It is therefore important to know where these breakpoints are in your application to make sure testing is done for each interval or use case.

Animations and Movement

Any content that conveys a sense of motion should be assessed. This can be a loader, video, synchronized media presentations (such as time-based interactive components and slideshows), animations, tickers, etc. Context, purpose, and implementation factor into how animations and moving elements should be handled, often aspects that cannot be tested via automated tooling. In general, support should be provided to start, stop, pause, or bypass any such content.

WCAG References

- Guideline 2.2: Enough Time

- Guideline 2.3: Seizures and Physical Reactions

Keyboard Accessibility

The ability to reach all content via keyboard is essential to accessibility. Many users with motor disabilities and vision impairments rely on keyboards (or other nonpointer devices) to navigate web sites and applications. Common potential issues include lack of focus indicators, focus traps, and tab order. Voice navigation (such as with a screen reader) may also be impacted by a lack of keyboard accessibility. Additionally, because screen readers often provide their own keyboard shortcuts, it's important to test keyboard accessibility both with and without a screen reader active to ensure access to all.

WCAG References

- Guideline 2.1: Keyboard Accessible

Focus Indicators

Although having style changes when an item is hovered over (with the mouse over the element) is quite common, having some indication of where the current focus is (selected element, typically by using the tab key), is much less common. Many browsers have defaults built-in for focus that are often user configurable but are often overridden for stylistic purposes and not replaced. Figure 4-11 shows a focus highlight in Firefox on the author's computer.

***Figure 4-11.** Focus highlight in Firefox*

In the preceding example, the focus is in the date field. It is important to note that the focus is denoted by more than just color. The outline width is also increased. This ensures that the focus will be visible even if the user is color blind.

WCAG References

- Success Criterion 1.4.1: Use of Color
- Success Criterion 2.4.7: Focus Visible

Tab Order

When going through a page focusable items (links, buttons, and form fields) need to be attainable while using only the keyboard. Focus should be able to be shifted from one to the next by hitting the "tab" key in order as they appear on the screen. In Figure 4-12, when tabbing through the form, the order should be

1. Name input

2. Date input

3. Submit button

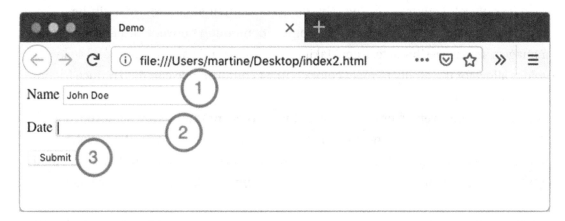

Figure 4-12. *Tab order*

WCAG References

- Success Criterion 1.4.1: Use of Color

- Success Criterion 2.4.3: Focus Order

Focus Traps

Even though focus can sometimes be restricted to a subsection of the content, such as in the context of a modal or dialog box, where the user should be limited to accessing items within the modal but not what is behind it, the user should always be able to exit the component. Focus traps occur when the user cannot navigate away from a subsection of content using keyboard navigation. This prevents keyboard users from being able to effectively navigate the application and should be avoided.

WCAG References

- Success Criterion 2.1.2: No Keyboard Trap

Color Contrast

Even though color contrast testing is based upon mathematics and can easily be automated, color choice can often be a point of contention between designers or brand managers and accessibility testing. Making sure that brand specifications and style guides allow for the ability to meet color contrast conformance can help reduce friction in future projects.

Furthermore, even when minimum color contrast minimums are achieved, it is important for color to never be the only differentiator between states. When color has a meaning, such as using red for error messages, the meaning also needs to be indicated by something else than color. Icons can be very helpful in this situation. See Figure 4-13.

Figure 4-13. *Error message denoted by both color and an icon*

WCAG References

- Success Criterion 1.4.1: Use of Color

- Success Criterion 1.4.3: Contrast (Minimum)

- Success Criterion 1.4.6: (Enhanced)

- Success Criterion 1.4.11: Non-text Contrast

Video and Audio Content

If the application contains video or audio content, these will require some combination of transcripts, audio descriptions, or captions based on the content.

Transcripts are a text-only version of the media's audio track, typically in document form. They can be used in multiple ways. They can be read either on screen or through assistive devices such as refreshable braille readers and screen readers. But they can also be searched and can be used for a quick glance to get an idea of what the media is about, or even for foreign-language translations.

Audio descriptions are a little different from transcripts. They are narrations added to describe important visual information that would not otherwise be conveyed via the transcript or context. For example, information about actions, or on screen text which would not normally be announced.

Captions are a text form of the audio information that is displayed on-screen, synchronized with the corresponding audio. They make audible content available to those who do not have access to audio and help users with comprehension as it allows the user to see the content as they hear it. Captions are essential when the visual information displayed in the video is tightly coupled to the audio track.

Although some automated testing tools can detect if these exist, what they cannot test for is if they are accurate and complete. Human testing will be necessary to verify that transcripts, audio descriptions, and captions are accurate and informative.

Additionally, audio content that plays automatically for more than 3 seconds should be pausable and/or have volume controls. The quality of the recording should also be assessed for background noise levels to ensure speech is easily discernible and understandable.

WCAG References

- Guideline 1.1: Text Alternatives

- Guideline 1.2: Time-based Media

- Success Criterion 1.4.2: Audio Control

- Success Criterion 1.4.7: Low or No Background Audio

Alternate Text

Similar to video needing a text description of the visual elements, images will require an alternative text, if they are relevant to the content and not just decorative. The following is a sample HTML image tag with alternate text:

```
<img src="kittens.png alt="Two cute white fluffy kittens playing with a
ball of purple yarn. Blue cursive letters at the bottom of the image read:
'Too Cute'">
```

Making sure that descriptions are relevant and convey all needed information is important to make sure users relying on them aren't missing out on any content. If text is included in the image, it should also be included in the alternate text description.

Most automated accessibility testing tools will be able to determine if the "alt" attribute is present on images but will not be able to test the quality of the description. This will have to be evaluated manually for each image. They also cannot determine the content of the image. Text content should not be presented as images unless the presentation of the text is essential to understanding the text, such as a logotype, or can be customized by the user. Note that even for decorative images an empty "alt" attribute must be provided and not simply omitted. This signals to the screen reader that the image is there for aesthetic purposes only and can be ignored.

WCAG References

- Guideline 1.1: Text Alternatives

- Success Criterion 1.4.5: Images of Text

Touchscreen Gestures

For many users, gestures such as swiping left and right, pinching to zoom, and even tapping to select are difficult or even impossible to execute. For example, a shake gesture would be incredibly cumbersome, if not impossible, for a user who has their device attached to their wheelchair. Gestures also have issues with discoverability, including a lack of on-screen indicators to signal that they exist. If the application includes gesture-activated actions, instruction on what the gestures are and what they do should be available to the users, and alternatives to gestures should be included in the app.

Audits

An audit usually includes a report for each page that includes a list of errors with which WCAG guidelines or criteria the error references. Resolution suggestions are sometimes also included.

The initial assessment may be performed as an audit, generating a report of changes needed to attain WCAG conformance. Often accessibility projects will involve multiple audits, and ideally audits should be repeated regularly – even on conforming applications – in order to ensure that the web site or application continues to meet guidelines and is free of defects.

Internal Audit

The preceding list of initial assessment considerations is not all-inclusive but is a good start to identifying the scope and nature of work, and determining what may need cross-department collaboration. If conducting an audit of the application internally it is still essential to have an accessibility expert to guide the testing and make sure that nothing is overlooked. Depending on the testers' accessibility experience, training may be required.

External Audit

External audits can be very beneficial because they provide an external set of eyes on the application and are done by experts who have extensive knowledge of assistive technologies and accessibility needs. These audits also gain the benefit of impartiality.

External audits are usually performed on a representative subset of pages with the understanding that findings will be applied to all pages. This provides a good base for what to look for everywhere in the application. Making sure that critical processes and pages of the application get included in the audit will help ensure accessibility of the application.

The audit usually generates a report for each page that includes a list of errors with which guidelines or criteria the error references. Resolution suggestions are sometimes also included.

Accessibility Testing

There are a wide variety of tools and techniques used to test for accessibility. For ease of discussion these have been split into three categories: Automated, Validators, and User Feedback.

Automated Testing

Some portions of testing can be done via automated tooling. These tools can be run via the command line, added to development and continuous integration pipelines, API based, or run as browser plug-ins.

One example of a browser plug-in tool is the Lighthouse[8] audit built into the Chrome developer tools. Lighthouse can audit more than just accessibility; it is therefore important to note that the accessibility checkbox is selected in the audit list. See Figure 4-14.

---

[8]https://developers.google.com/web/tools/lighthouse/.

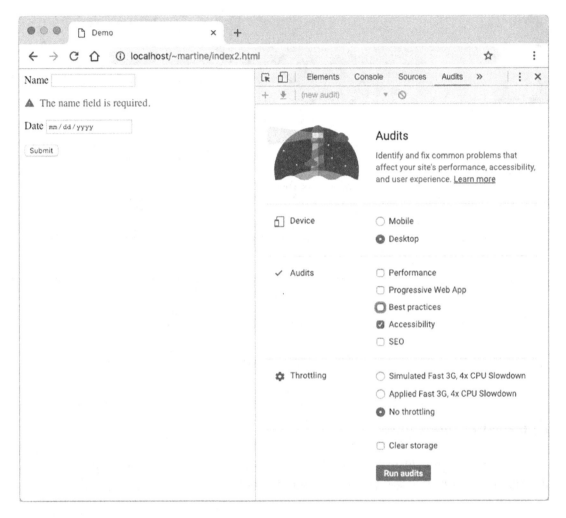

Figure 4-14. *Lighthouse audit tools*

When running an audit with automatic tooling, most will give a list of errors which include the violation, where in the code it appears, and a link to documentation which usually references the specific requirement and success criteria being violated.

In addition, some tools will also list what they were unable to test for that will require manual testing (Figure 4-15).

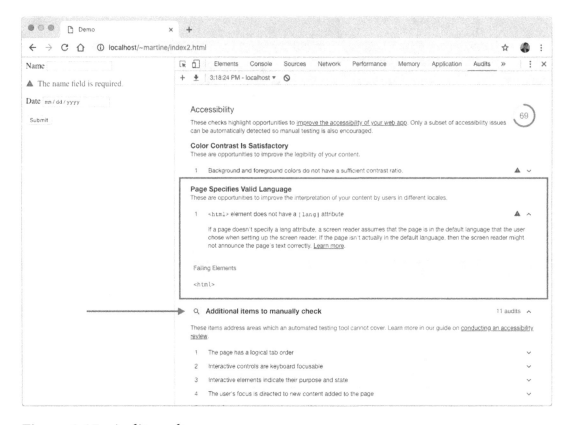

Figure 4-15. *Audit results*

A list of additional testing tools can be found on W3C WAI's Web Accessibility Evaluation Tools List at www.w3.org/WAI/ER/tools/.

Validators

HTML that is coded following the HTML specification is an important first step to making the website or web application accessible. Accessibility becomes hindered when styles and scripting are added without consideration of user needs. Making sure that the application's HTML, whether written or generated, follows the HTML specification can help resolve issues right from the start. Markup validators can be used to automatically check the code.

Notice the warning for the language attribute in Figure 4-16. It was flagged as an accessibility error in Figure 4-15.

Figure 4-16. *HTML validator results*[9]

User Feedback

No matter how many automated tools are leveraged, user testing and feedback are still critical to ensuring that all content is usable. Whether accessibility is being assessed internally or by an external agency, it is important to verify that any resolutions made to correct accessibility shortcomings were effective. Even if all the specifications and rules are followed to the letter, a page or interaction may not be clear. It is therefore critical to solicit user feedback and to provide them with an avenue to do so when they are engaging with the application.

At the end of the day, all of the tools and specifications exist to help guide an application in the correct direction. Conformance is a matter of documentation and best effort, but true accessibility exists only within the ability of each and every user to access information and accomplish tasks.

---

[9]https://validator.w3.org/#validate_by_uri.

Summary

In this chapter we have covered how to assess the scope of testing that will be performed and what to consider during initial assessment. This includes areas that will need manual intervention and potential cross discipline collaboration. You have learned about:

- The role of Accessibility Statements in an accessibility initiative
- Reviewing a web site or web application for complete accessibility coverage
- Performing automated assessments with Lighthouse
- Manually reviewing keyboard accessibility

In the next chapter we will present a roadmap you can use to make an application accessible, and keep it that way.

CHAPTER 5

Creating an Action Plan

This chapter will describe how to create a step-by-step roadmap for your new and existing web applications, which in turn will help you achieve and maintain conformance to accessibility standards. Finally, two sample scenarios are presented to illustrate how the roadmap can be created and applied to your team.

Roadmap

Once the application has been analyzed for critical paths and the accessibility level has been determined, you're ready to begin getting the application conformant and made accessible to the users. Just as important as improving the accessibility of your current applications is making sure that a process is in place so that future development also conforms to WCAG and accessibility best practices so as to maintain accessibility long term.

While the action plan is laid out in phases, it is not meant to be a project plan, but rather a roadmap to guide the reader toward an accessible project (Figure 5-1). This roadmap can then be applied to many forms of project management, including lean, agile, and waterfall.

© Martine Dowden and Michael Dowden 2019
M. Dowden and M. Dowden, *Approachable Accessibility*, https://doi.org/10.1007/978-1-4842-4881-2_5

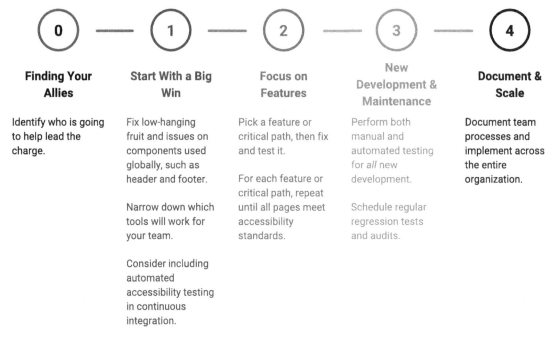

Figure 5-1. Action plan phases

Phase 0: Finding Your Allies

Finding Your Allies

Identify who is going to help lead the charge.

In any team, each member will have different experiences and motivations, leading to a wide variety of reactions to being approached about making an application accessible. They may see it as something great that will help their users, or more work that is piled onto their already full plate, and any reaction in between. If this person has never been involved with an accessibility project, they will need to learn a whole new body of information, which can also be daunting. It will be helpful at this point to understand which team members will "champion the cause," and which ones are going to need some extra motivation or training. While you can certainly get started on your own, having support from your team will make this easier.

QUESTIONS TO ASK

- What is my team's skill level and awareness of accessibility?

- Does anyone want or need training?

- Do timelines need to be adjusted to account for the learning curve?

- What responsibilities will each person have?

    - Making development changes

    - Testing changes and conformance to standards

    - Writing documentation

This is also a great time to start considering which automated testing tools the team wants to use and start experimenting with them. Each tool will have its own way of working and quirks that take time to learn. Experimenting and playing with them will help the team find the one(s) that will work the best with their workflow and development process. (See Chapter 6 for more details around tool selection.)

Running an automated testing tool, such as the Chrome browser plug-in Axe[1] on pages that will be focused on first, is a great way to get a baseline idea of the work to be done. Even though it is only a partial view into the problems, it will expose some easy-to-fix errors that can be started with. It also provides a metric for showing progress in the right direction by showing that the number of errors is decreasing.

---

[1] https://chrome.google.com/webstore/detail/axe/lhdoppojpmngadmnindnejefpokejbdd?hl=en-US.

Phase 1: Start with a Big Win

Start With a Big Win

Fix low hanging fruit and issues on components used globally, such as header and footer.

Narrow down which tools will work for your team.

Consider including automated accessibility testing in continuous integration.

As mentioned earlier, starting a new project which requires learning a whole new body of knowledge can be intimidating. Being confronted with what looks like hundreds of errors can also be very overwhelming. Starting gently with some easy fixes, or going for fixes with global impact, can both produce big wins that will help get team members familiar with the accessibility specification, how the tools work, and what types of changes they will be making. For many types of errors, once a solution has been identified, there is a high likelihood that it can be replicated throughout the application. It is very common for the same type of error to be found multiple times in any application as developers often use patterns for solving specific problems. An example of such a task would be adding missing alt tags to images. These kinds of errors can easily be tested for in the browser using browser plug-ins or using code analysis tools. Furthermore, many of these tools, along with the error, will indicate the specific WCAG criteria that is being violated and possible solutions.

At this stage it is also helpful to look at errors in areas that are repeated throughout the application. In component-based architecture, a feature, UI component, or "widget" will be coded once and then reused, or "dropped in" multiple times throughout the site. If the application has a header, footer, or main navigation, these areas are often found on every page. Tackling errors being generated in those areas first will have a very large impact quickly. Furthermore, once they are dealt with, focus can be shifted to individual features and pages without the noise of the same errors showing up over and over again across pages for those areas.

While knocking out the first tasks, it is a good time to narrow down and settle on the set of tools the team will use to do automated testing. These tools will be used by developers to spot check as they code and for debugging, and by testers to validate that errors have been resolved. At this point, the focus is not on perfection but on making sure the number of errors is diminishing, and that no new errors are being introduced. Manual testing using assistive technologies should also start at this point in the process.

CONTINUOUS INTEGRATION AND DEPLOYMENT (CI/CD)

At any time from this point forward, automated accessibility testing can be added to the continuous integration. Having accessibility testing integrated as part of the build and deploy process, much like unit or integration tests, will help solidify accessibility as a normal part of development, rather than as an add-on criteria. Furthermore, it will help maintain the accessibility status of the application.

Especially if the application being worked on is continuously deployed, this is a good time to add an accessibility statement to the application. Even though the application is not accessible yet, it will inform the users that accessibility is now a priority and that issues are actively being worked on. As more pieces of the application are fixed, the statement will need to be updated with the progress being made. This will reinforce with the users that accessibility is, in fact, being taken seriously and provide a point of contact for asking questions and reporting issues. As pieces get fixed and are stated to be accessible, this will give users a conduit to communicate with the team if something has been missed, or if the implementation still needs to be adjusted to make the user experience even better.

QUESTIONS TO ASK

- What components are repeated on multiple pages?
- When running automated tools, what are some errors that seemed to be frequently repeated?
- Do all of the images have meaningful alternate text?
- Does my color palette meet accessibility guidelines for contrast?

Understanding who the users are, and how they are using the application, is important to making the application not merely meet the target specification, but to become a truly usable and enjoyable experience for all.

Phase 2: Focus on Features

Focus on Features

Pick a feature or critical path, then fix and test it.

For each feature or critical path, repeat until all pages meet accessibility standards.

By this phase, the team should start having a pretty good idea about which processes and tools work for them. Making a decision on which tools and techniques will be used for testing – and making sure it is documented – will help the designers, developers, and testers alike. It will help solidify a process, and the consistency will make it so that errors are easier to reproduce. Using the same tools will also allow tracking the number of bugs still left to make sure that the number is in fact going down, and that no new errors are being introduced.

Once the global and reusable portions of the applications have been addressed, it becomes much easier to focus on specific features. With errors in repeated portions of the application like the header or footer out of the way, the errors left are those of the specific page or feature. The advantage of focusing on a feature or path is that areas, or actions, of the application can become accessible gradually for the user. If errors are fixed disjointedly, a user may not be able to use the application at all until the work is entirely finished. If development follows features, then even if a user cannot use the entire application, they may still be able to accomplish some tasks which is often better than no access at all.

TALKING TO THE EXPERTS

The low-hanging fruit have been taken care of, and the more in-depth testing of keyboard navigation, focus traps, and screen reader support, are now under way. If the team does not have an experienced accessibility person available to them, bringing in an expert to help guide development and testing can be a huge asset to the team. Areas this person can help with include industry best practices, testing techniques, coding techniques, assistive technologies, and general knowledge about the specification itself.

This phase will continue until all features of the application have been assessed, fixed, and tested both programmatically and manually. Even if elements such as headers and footers were already fixed as part of Phase 1, testing them again in the context of a full feature regression will help expose interaction issues. These may include interpage keyboard navigation, screen reader behavior, and impact of timed elements. These types of interactions cannot be tested through code analysis and cannot be assessed when elements are tested in isolation rather than as part of a larger page or process. A sample feature implementation cycle for creating or fixing accessible features is shown in Figure 5-2.

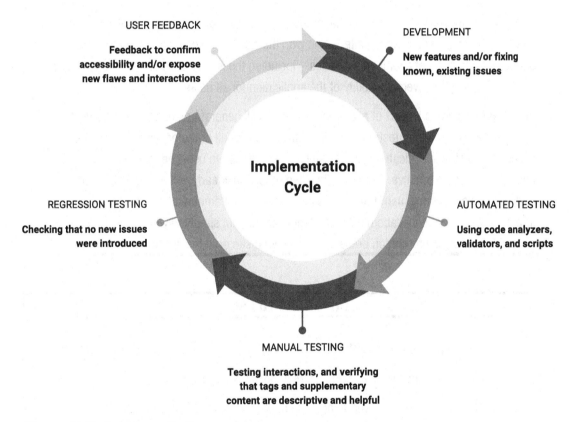

Figure 5-2. *Implementation cycle*

As features are made accessible, the accessibility statement will need to be updated to reflect the progress being made. Incorporating user feedback will also help make using the application easier and more usable for the user.

FOCUS GROUPS

User research is a very effective way to improve the usability and accessibility of an application or web site. Users may not use the application in the way it was intended or expected. New features may go ignored – not because they are not valuable, but because they are not discoverable, and users are unaware that they exist. While analytics can show a lack of use, it cannot as easily explain why. Furthermore, users may be annoyed by certain aspects of the application or have ideas for improvement that the development team or business stakeholders have not thought of.

To capture that feedback, a more formal group of users can be formed from which specific feedback is requested, or whose interaction with the app is observed for pain points. Making sure to include users of a variety of abilities – including those that use assistive technologies – will help improve the overall usability of the application for all users.

Including focus group as part of accessibility testing will generate feedback not otherwise attainable through regular testing. Even if a feature checks all of the boxes to be considered accessible per the specifications, it may still be very difficult to use. The interaction may be cumbersome or nonintuitive. Receiving this kind of feedback early will help development understand how to implement future fixes and decrease the amount of rework necessary. It is important to be intentional about soliciting feedback and not simply relying on user feedback through the contact information presented on the web site or in the accessibility statement.

QUESTIONS TO ASK

- What are my user demographics?

- What analytics are we collecting and what does it tell us?

- What devices are being used to access our web sites and applications?

- What context or circumstance are users in when they are using the application? (Noisy subway while commuting to work? At home, on their desktop computer?)

- Do we have user feedback regarding our application? What does it say?

- Is our application available in multiple languages? Do we need to make sure that alt attributes, aria attributes, descriptions, and the like are also available in multiple languages?

- Do I have different types of users that may use the application differently based on their role (child using a tablet to learn spelling words vs. teacher setting up the spelling list for the week on a laptop)?

Phase 3: Development and Maintenance

3

New Development & Maintenance

Perform both manual and automated testing for *all* new development.

Schedule regular regression tests and audits.

Congratulations, you made it! Your application is now accessible. Take a moment to celebrate, but unfortunately you don't get to relax forever.

EXTERNAL AUDIT

This is a great time to request an external audit to double-check that nothing has been missed. Results from the audit make great educational tools and teaching cases for the team. In much the same way that financial audits are performed by outside companies, this audit should be performed by a consultant or an outside firm that specializes in accessibility testing and conformance. Using a third party for this audit helps ensure it is independent and objective.

Maintaining accessibility is all about continually testing and obtaining feedback from real users. With any new feature that is developed, the acceptance criteria should also include any accessibility criteria and expectations and be tested accordingly. Regular integration and regression testing are also crucial to maintenance. In Phase 1, continuous integration is mentioned. If accessibility testing has not been included in the project's build and deploy pipeline yet, it is strongly recommended to add it in now. This will help ensure that the tests are being run and keep accessibility front of mind throughout the entire development cycle, rather than becoming the thing that is cobbled together at the end. Furthermore, it normalizes accessibility as part of the team's everyday process and responsibility.

Continuing education is also important to maintaining the application's accessibility. New devices are created every day, and the Internet is constantly evolving, technology becomes obsolete, and specifications are updated and expanded. The specification documents are living records that are regularly updated. Keeping tabs on the WCAG specification itself is important, but conferences, webinars, user groups, and articles, as well as getting involved in the accessibility community, are also great ways to stay current.

QUESTIONS TO ASK

- Have my user demographics changed?

- Are my users still using the same devices and technologies?

- What are users saying about the product?

- Have legal requirements changed?

- How do my preconformance metrics compare with today's metrics?

Phase 4: Document and Scale

Document & Scale

Document team processes and implement across the entire organization.

Having gone through the process of making an application accessible, lessons learned and knowledge acquired should be shared with the rest of the organization. Documenting process, hurdles, and solutions is a great way to give other teams a head start on making their projects accessible. To scale the process out, educating the organization about the need for accessibility is also important. If the data is available, show the returns on investment such as customer satisfaction rating, increased number of users, etc. Compelling numbers can be a great motivator to get the organization on board. Also be sure to share any stories you collect from users, both during focus groups and any you obtain through the web site. Recounting personal tales of success and frustration can go a long way to driving home the importance of improving the accessibility web sites and applications.

Now we'll see examples of how this roadmap can be applied to your team; two scenarios are presented: one featuring a small team and another featuring a large company.

Scenario 1: A Small Team with a New Project

A new startup company is beginning development on an all-new product. The team is comprised of a CEO, two developers (one front-end, one back-end), a designer (who is also responsible for marketing), and a systems engineer (Figure 5-3).

Figure 5-3. *The team*

In researching their target market, the CEO realizes that their new web application must be accessible in order to serve their entire target market.

Phase 0: Finding Your Allies

The CEO presents the findings to the team and challenges them to make the new application accessible right out of the gate. Even though none of the team members have much experience with accessibility, they agree to do the work required to learn what will be involved. After reviewing the guidelines they decide to target WCAG AA as their conformance level. As far as they know, they have no other legal requirements regarding accessibility.

Phase 1: Start with a Big Win

Because it is a brand new project, there are not yet any issues to fix! The goal is to make sure it stays that way, so the front-end developer and designer work hand in hand to choose colors, font sizes, and plan out content structure and layout. As development starts, the team experiments with tools and uses the errors generated by them to learn about the WCAG specifications and how to maintain conformance. The team starts development by building their own UI elements from scratch, but based upon what they see from the accessibility tools, they quickly decide to adopt a standard library.

Phase 2: Focus on Features

As they get more comfortable with the tools and testing, and with the WCAG specification, they settle on a set of automated tools. The code analyzer they choose has both a browser plug-in and a downloadable version. This appeals to them because they can use the browser version for spot checking while they are coding, and the downloaded version can be added to the continuous integration and deployment pipeline. Additionally, the designer and systems engineer help with the manual testing. They focus a lot on trying to use their application on different devices, and without using a mouse. An accessibility statement is included in the first release.

Phase 3: Development and Maintenance

Because no one on the team has much experience with accessibility, the CEO orders an external audit of their application. The audit comes back with errors exposing a gap in what they are testing, and some odds and ends they had missed. They fix the issues, but also use the results as a teaching tool and opportunity to research what they had missed. In doing so they realize that they had misunderstood some of the WCAG criteria and updated their tests and processes to prevent future problems as a result. They continue to do regular external audits of the application – especially after major feature releases – and to seek out user feedback to make sure they remain accessible.

Phase 4: Document and Scale

Because they are planning to grow rapidly and begin expanding the team, they begin documenting their processes, decisions, and architecture. As the team grows, they continue to learn more about accessibility via conferences, training, and user feedback. As new members are added to the team, because accessibility is already a core component of the organization's processes, it is easily accepted by new members of the team.

Scenario 2: A Big Organization with Many Large Products

A large financial services company, headquartered in a large downtown skyscraper, supports a large number of web sites and web applications. These applications serve customers, partners, vendors, and employees alike. One product team of 14 people (Figure 5-4) is responsible for ongoing maintenance and support of a mission-critical application used by several of their important corporate clients.

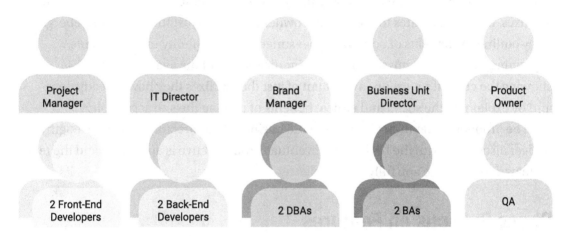

Figure 5-4. *The team*

Phase 0: Finding Your Allies

An enthusiastic business analyst (BA) returns from a conference at which they attended a talk about accessibility. They are excited about improving the product, and fresh with information about the hurdles disabled users face online, and want to implement improvements on the application. While talking with the team about their newfound knowledge, they attract the attention of one of the back-end developers, who is eager to help. It turns out the developer's child is hearing impaired, and they are familiar with some of the challenges involved in interfacing with technology.

To get an idea of the pain points in the application, the BA adds some accessibility questions to the user surveys and user interviews already scheduled with the clients. This exposes a number of keyboard accessibility issues, especially regarding forms. Another common complaint is that the application does not work well on mobile devices. It is neither fluid nor responsive, and some of the features such as drag and drop elements don't work with touch at all. The complaints are logged, and new tasks are created to address the issues.

Phase 1: Start with a Big Win

As the reported user experience issues get fixed and deployed, user satisfaction ratings increase. The business unit director also notices that the number of support calls related to the application has decreased. Using the success and momentum gained by the first few fixes, the BA advocates to the product owner that this is just the tip of the iceberg. They outline the benefits of additional investment in accessibility improvements, explaining that they are missing out on a significant part of the available market – showing the current return on investment of just the few fixes they have already done – and by explaining the social and ethical benefits of making the site accessible.

The product owner then takes this to the business unit director, who has a lengthy budget discussion with the IT director. Eventually the directive is approved, and the team is cleared to make the app fully accessible.

Phase 2: Focus on Features

The attorneys are enlisted to help write an accessibility statement to be added to the application, while the front-end developers work with the brand manager to figure out how they will alter the color scheme to make sure it conforms to WCAG AA. The BAs work on adding accessibility criteria to existing development tasks, and the tester researches how testing will be affected.

The tester raises concerns about the added workload that is created by not only testing functionality, but now adding accessibility testing on top of this. The back-end developer who was very excited about this project offers to help with testing to keep things moving forward. They start by getting on the phone with the operations team and have automated testing added to the build and deploy pipeline to make sure a first pass is completed before QA even has to look at it.

User satisfaction continues to increase and support call volume to decrease, but the team does get reports from a screen reader user that the application still doesn't work quite right. Finding themselves a bit out of their depth, they get approval from the IT Director to hire a consultant specializing in accessibility, who helps guide them through the necessary fixes and issues, while training them on screen reader support.

Phase 3: Development and Maintenance

With a first round of success under their belt, accessibility has become integrated into the team's process. New development is being done with accessibility in mind from the beginning, which the team finds much easier to handle than retrofitting previous work. The business owner continues to track the return on investment with positive results. The team continues to learn more about accessibility both from the consultant and from experience.

Phase 4: Document and Scale

Accessibility now firmly ingrained as part of this team's process, and business management having noticed the benefits adding accessibility has brought, the BAs approach management about helping other teams in the organization do the same. With the help of the consultant, the BAs document the process they went through to make the application accessible, and how they handle new development and testing now. One by one, teams start being trained and adopting accessibility until it becomes standard as part of the corporate process.

Summary

In this chapter we have presented the outline for creating your own action plan to improve the accessibility of your applications, and to integrate the team into your initiatives. This was illustrated with two different scenarios including small and large teams, and both new and existing products. Along the way you've learned

- Questions to ask when building your team and planning your project
- The importance of combining both automated and manual testing
- The role experts and focus groups can play in your initiatives
- Steps to maintaining the accessibility of a web site or web application

In the following chapter, you will learn about the tools available to help with your accessibility testing and implementation, technology being used by your users, and resources for further research.

CHAPTER 6

Tools, Technologies, and Resources

This chapter will provide an overview of the types of tools and resources you will need to complete your accessibility initiatives. The goal is to highlight the types of tools available, how to use them within your teams and projects, and where to go for additional information.

There are a great number of tools available which are not covered here. This is intended to be a categorical overview, including tools with which the authors are familiar.

The WAI maintains a very lengthy list of tools at `www.w3.org/WAI/ER/tools/` which cannot be covered here. When reviewing tools you will discover that while many are free, there are also a large number of commercial tools available.

The tools presented here are not being endorsed in any way, but they serve as examples of a category of tools. Also, the quality and relevance of any given tool is subject to rapid change. Please research each tool you intend to use and make the best decision for your team's specific goals.

Development Tools

These tools are for developers and testers alike to assist with implementation and quality assurance of web accessibility.

Validators

When attempting to build an accessible web site or web application, the very first and most important step is to make sure that the markup and code you are writing has valid code syntax. Any errors in coding, and the browsers and assistive technology won't be

© Martine Dowden and Michael Dowden 2019
M. Dowden and M. Dowden, *Approachable Accessibility*, https://doi.org/10.1007/978-1-4842-4881-2_6

able to correctly parse and interpret the content, layout, or choices available to the user. This is necessary to provide a robust and accessible code base.

As mentioned in Chapter 4, one way to perform this validation is using the traditional W3C web-based validators.

W3C Markup Validation Service

The Markup Validation Service[1] shown in Figure 6-1 allows you to provide HTML content via URL, File Upload, or Direct Input (copy-and-paste).

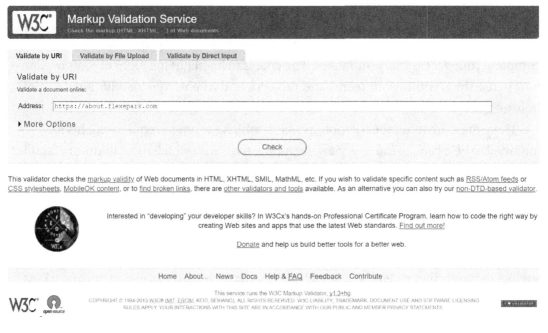

Figure 6-1. *Markup validation service*

Ideally the results will come back clean, but the first time you run the tool you're likely to get a number of warnings and errors. In Figure 6-2 there are a few warnings, but nothing that would pose a problem for accessibility.

---

[1]https://validator.w3.org/.

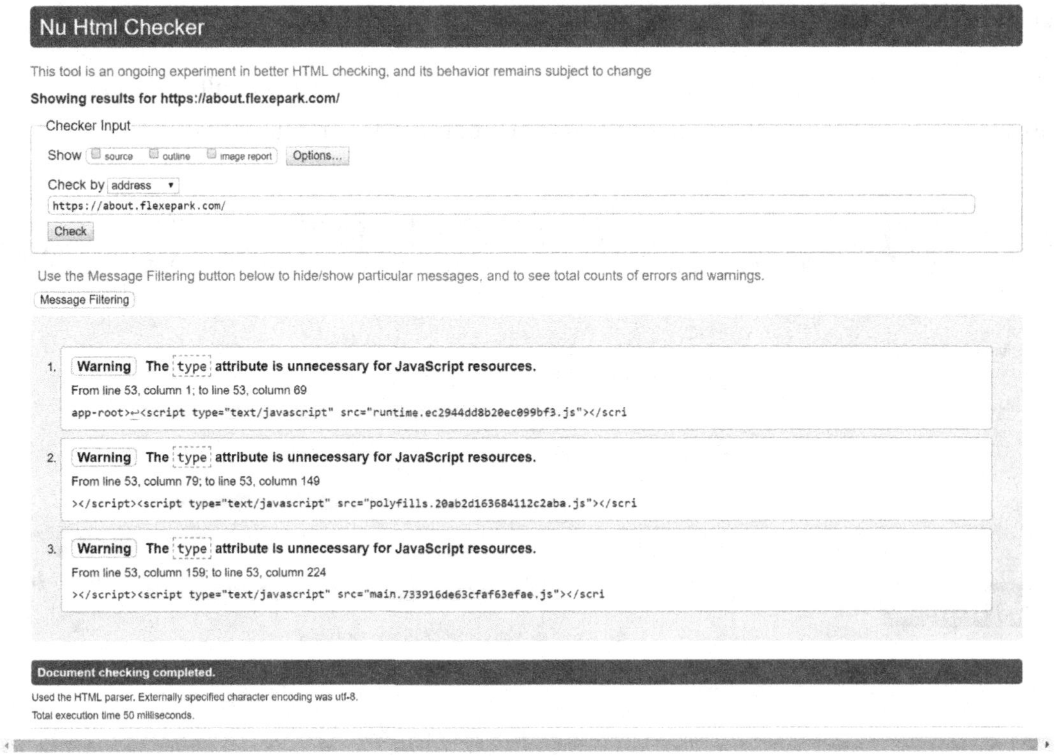

Nu Html Checker

This tool is an ongoing experiment in better HTML checking, and its behavior remains subject to change

Showing results for https://about.flexepark.com/

Checker Input

Show ☐ source ☐ outline ☐ image report   Options...

Check by address ▼

https://about.flexepark.com/

Check

Use the Message Filtering button below to hide/show particular messages, and to see total counts of errors and warnings.

Message Filtering

1.   **Warning**   The `type` attribute is unnecessary for JavaScript resources.
     From line 53, column 1; to line 53, column 69
     app-root>↵<script type="text/javascript" src="runtime.ec2944dd8b20ec099bf3.js"></scri

2.   **Warning**   The `type` attribute is unnecessary for JavaScript resources.
     From line 53, column 79; to line 53, column 149
     ></script><script type="text/javascript" src="polyfills.20ab2d163684112c2aba.js"></scri

3.   **Warning**   The `type` attribute is unnecessary for JavaScript resources.
     From line 53, column 159; to line 53, column 224
     ></script><script type="text/javascript" src="main.733916de63cfaf63efae.js"></scri

Document checking completed.

Used the HTML parser. Externally specified character encoding was utf-8.
Total execution time 50 milliseconds.

Figure 6-2. *Markup validation results*

Note that while you can use this tool manually, there are a number of variations of the checker intended for command line or continuous integration use. See the Nu Html Checker web site[2] for more information.

Note   All tools have limitations and purposes for which they were built. When choosing a tool make sure you know what those are. For example, Nu Html Checker specifically states in their documentation that:

"The Nu Html Checker should not be used as a means to attempt to unilaterally enforce pass/fail conformance of documents to any particular specifications; it is intended solely as a checker, not as a pass/fail certification mechanism."[2]

---

[2]https://validator.w3.org/nu/about.html.

W3C CSS Validation Service

Similar to the HTML service, The CSS Validation Service[3] (Figure 6-3) allows you to provide CSS content via URL, File Upload, or Direct Input (copy-and-paste).

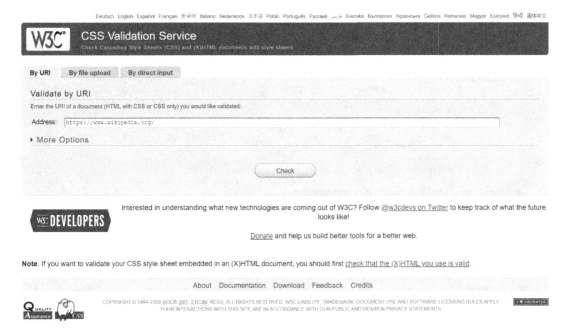

Figure 6-3. *CSS Validation Service*

When the CSS is clean and error-free, you not only get a friendly message of congratulations, you are told exactly what CSS level your page supports and even presented with valid CSS buttons you can include on your web site like it's 1998 again. See Figure 6-4.

---

[3]https://jigsaw.w3.org/css-validator/.

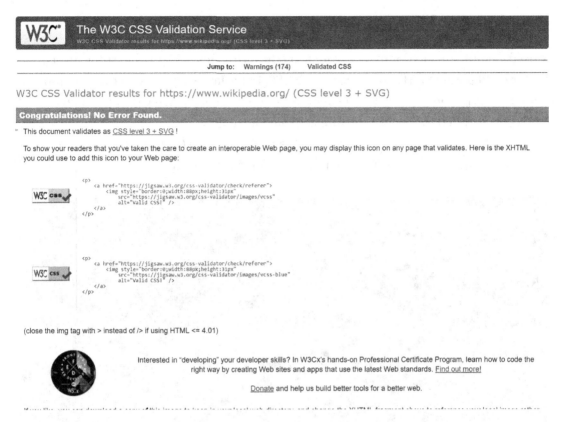

Figure 6-4. *CSS validation results*

Note that even if no errors are found, there may be a long list of warnings, particularly in the case of vendor-specific extensions or pseudo-elements. This tool remains mostly useful for manually spot-checking pages or files, although it is downloadable[4] as a Java command-line utility.

If using a CSS precompiler such as SASS, LESS, or Stylus, the need for CSS validation is diminished as most errors will prevent the CSS from being compiled. However, spot checking that vendor-specific markup is present can be useful for cross-browser compatibility.

---

[4]https://jigsaw.w3.org/css-validator/DOWNLOAD.html.

Development Environment

Most development environments, from text editors to IDEs, will provide some level of syntax highlighting for HTML, CSS, SASS/SCSS, LESS, JavaScript, and TypeScript (among others). This provides you with excellent real-time feedback when writing new code, and it is recommended to keep this feature activated at all times.

In the following example (Figure 6-5), Visual Studio (VS) Code is using red text and underline to mark errors, and green underlines to mark warnings.

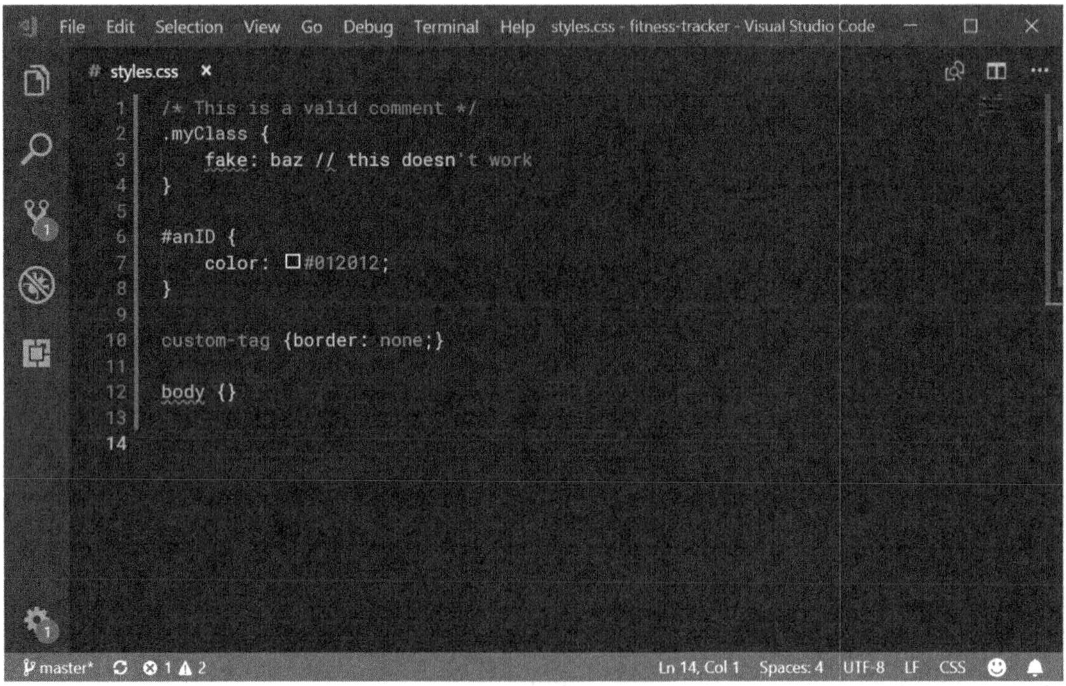

Figure 6-5. *CSS highlighting in VS Code*

In the next example (Figure 6-6), the HTMLHint extension[5] uses a similar set of markings to indicate errors and warnings in an HTML file.

---

[5]`https://marketplace.visualstudio.com/items?itemName=mkaufman.HTMLHint.`

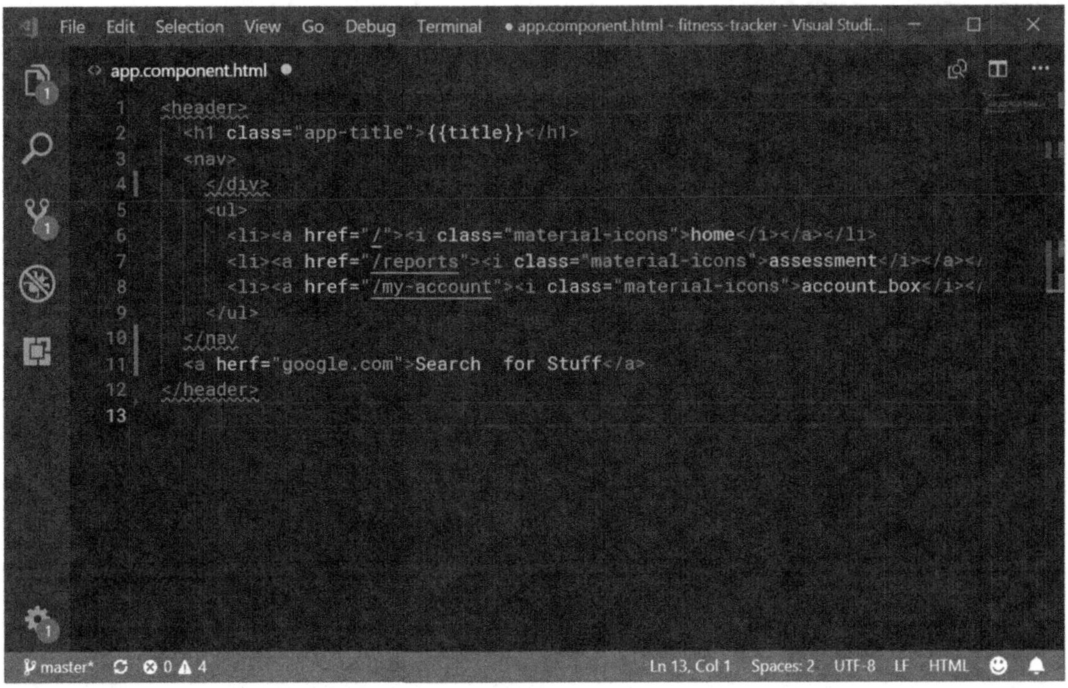

Figure 6-6. *HTML highlighting in VS Code*

Command Line

For automation, however, nothing serves your purposes better than a Command Line Interface (CLI) validator. There are many options, but some popular choices include those listed on Table 6-1.

Table 6-1. *Command Line Validators*

Language	Tool	URL
CSS	stylelint	https://stylelint.io/
HTML	HTMLHint	https://github.com/htmlhint/HTMLHint
JavaScript	ESLint	https://eslint.org/
TypeScript	TSLint	https://palantir.github.io/tslint/

Used together within your build process, these tools are capable of automatically checking for formatting and syntax errors that can cause problems down the line with accessibility and can help prevent bugs at the same time. This can be implemented at any time but should definitely be completed by Phase 3 in your Action Plan as indicated in Chapter 5.

Testing Tools

While important, clean code is just the beginning. Testing the quality and structure of our content, and the conformance to WCAG, are also essential to ensuring consistency in our support for accessibility.

When using the following tools, please note that they mainly operate one page at a time. In order to fully test your entire site, you'll need to run the tool on every single page.

Content Testing

One of the primary goals of accessibility is to make content available to all. Therefore, the content itself is as important as its structure. Considerations of audio, video, and animation content, as well as color contrast, have all been discussed in Chapters 1 and 4. But textual content may also need to be reviewed.

The structure and word choice in your textual content can reduce accessibility to the information. Education level, reading ability, and cognitive or neurological disabilities may all factor into the ability for a person to comprehend the content on your web site or application.

The **Readability Test Tool**,[6] shown in Figure 6-7, can help you ensure that the reading level of your content is appropriate to your audience. The tool can be embedded on your web page but, like the validators mentioned earlier, you can also run it directly via URL or Direct Input.

---

[6]www.webfx.com/tools/read-able/.

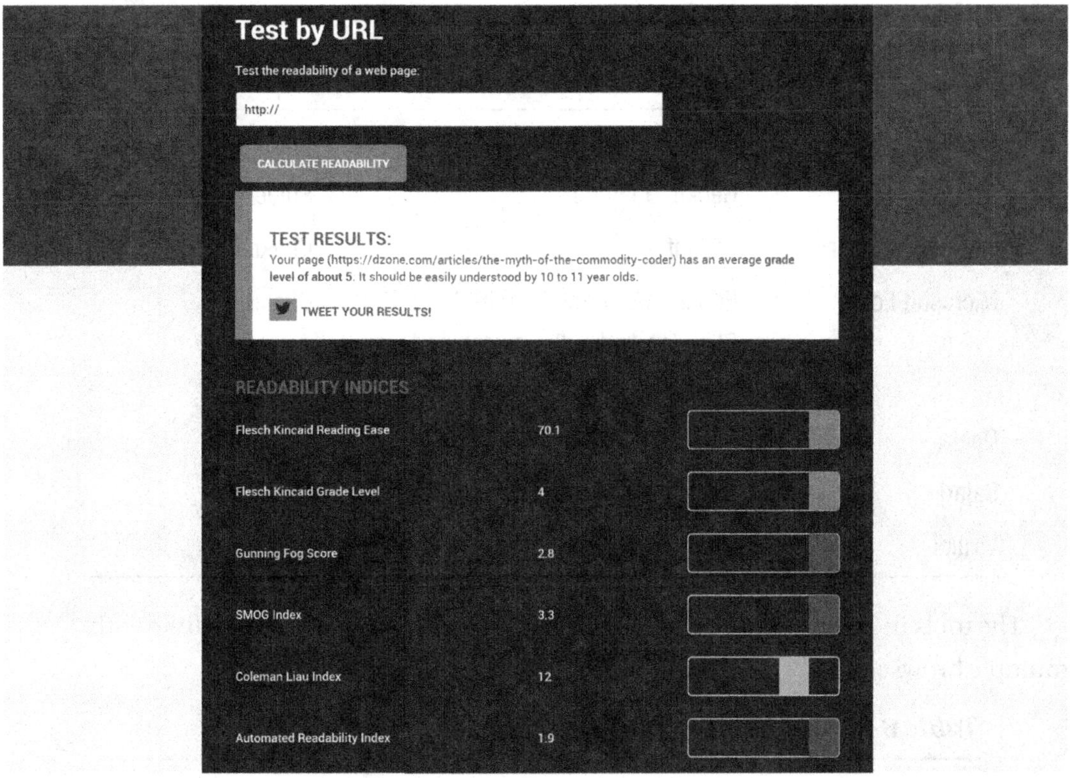

Figure 6-7. *Readability report*

Conformance Testing

While we can't entirely replace manual testing, there are a large number of success criteria tests that can be automated. The tools presented in this section handle this task in a variety of ways. Typically, these tools will run in a browser, either manually or through a headless browser (a browser without a graphical interface, usually run via a command line), in order to evaluate a page in its full context. Because of this, cross-browser support may become a critical issue for your accessibility projects.

It is important to test the application for both compatibility and accessibility in multiple browsers, because they do not all use the same layout and JavaScript engines, which leads to variation in how they interpret code. Table 6-2 lists some common browsers and their engines.

Table 6-2. *Browser Technology*

Browser	Layout Engine	JavaScript Engine
Chrome	Blink (Chromium), WebKit (on iOS)	Chrome V8
Firefox	Gecko, Quantum	SpiderMonkey
Internet Explorer	Trident	Chakra
Microsoft Edge	EdgeHTML, WebKit (on iOS), Blink (on Android) – switching to a Chromium platform[7]	Chakra
Opera	Blink (Chromium)	Chrome V8
Safari	WebKit	Nitro
Vivaldi	Blink (Chromium)	Chrome V8

The tools in Table 6-3 are browser based, several of which are compatible with multiple browsers.

Table 6-3. *Accessibility Testing Tools*

Tool	URL
Tota11y	http://khan.github.io/tota11y/
Wave	https://wave.webaim.org/extension/
Axe	www.deque.com/axe/
Lighthouse	https://developers.google.com/web/tools/lighthouse/
pa11y	http://pa11y.org/

Visualization

If you're just getting started with web accessibility, one of the challenges is understanding how a browser or assistive technology sees the web page. Tools that overlay accessibility information over the existing content can be extremely helpful in understanding what's going on behind the scenes.

---

[7]https://blogs.windows.com/windowsexperience/2018/12/06/microsoft-edge-making-the-web-better-through-more-open-source-collaboration/.

Tota11y

The **Tota11y**[8] visualization tool from Khan Academy is very interactive, allowing you to choose what is highlighted, while continuing to interact with the page normally. Tota11y is a simple JavaScript file that can be embedded on your pages. It can also be installed as a bookmarklet, allowing you to run the tool without including it directly on the page. See Figure 6-8.

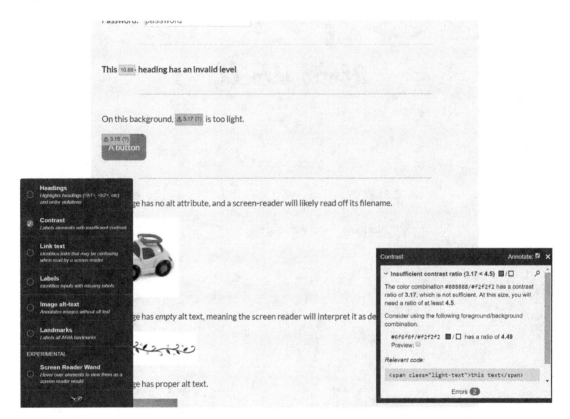

Figure 6-8. *Tota11y contrast plug-in*

---

[8]http://khan.github.io/tota11y/.

WAVE

WebAIM's **WAVE**[9] (Web Accessibility Evaluation Tool) can also provide visualizations on the page. Running the browser extension adds visual "tags" to the page which can be interacted with for additional information. Figure 6-9 shows the wave toolbar to the left of the web page. The tool overlays markers to show significant structure items such as the navigation, headers, and alternative text.

Figure 6-9. *WAVE summary*

The output is highly configurable, including selecting by conformance level or even excluding individual guidelines or success criteria. Figure 6-10 shows the individual categories expanded. Each category (Errors, Alerts, Features, Structural Elements, HTM5 and ARIA, Color Contrast Errors) can be selected to show visual indicators of the element or error on the page or deselected to hide the indicators and reduce distraction.

---

[9]https://wave.webaim.org/extension/.

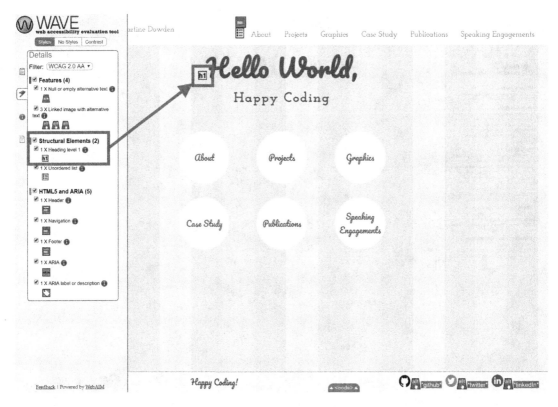

Figure 6-10. *WAVE filter*

When reviewing the results, selecting information icon ❶ will take you to documentation on the success criteria straight from WCAG, including links directly to the relevant WCAG guidelines and criterion. Figure 6-11 shows the wave browser plug-in's documentation view.

Figure 6-11. *WAVE documentation*

Assessment

While exploratory assessments and visual assessment of the page are extremely useful during development, these methods would be extremely labor intensive to use as the primary mode of evaluating conformance on a continuing basis.

Axe

Deque **axe**[10] is an open source rules library for accessibility testing. While the library is available for you to integrate into your own projects and custom tools, the most common way to use axe is through one of the supported browser extensions. Once installed in Chrome, for example, you access axe through its own tab in the DevTools. Simply load up the web page you want to test and click Analyze. Figure 6-12 shows the Axe tab in the dev tools ready to analyze the page.

---

[10]www.deque.com/axe/.

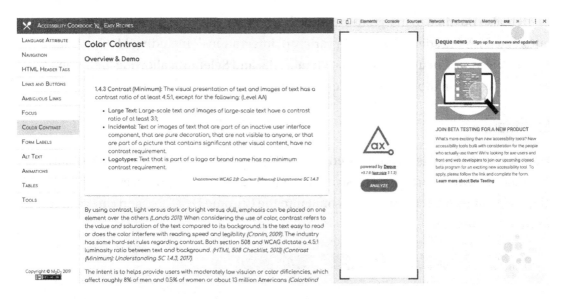

Figure 6-12. *Axe*

After running the analysis, you receive a list of issues, which can be filtered by type. There are arrows for navigating between issues (which will highlight them in the browser window) and specific information about the violation and the code that caused the issue. Clicking the "learn more" link will open a page of documentation which includes WCAG success criteria as seen in Figure 6-13.

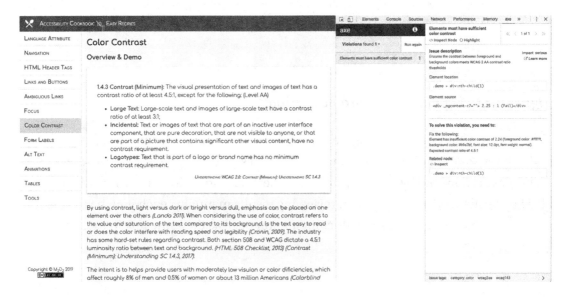

Figure 6-13. *Axe report*

It is also possible to integrate axe directly into your continuous integration or automated testing suite. There are a variety of integrations[11] including Mocha, Jest, Jasmine, Karma, Cucumber, Jenkins, PhantomJS, and Selenium allowing for automated, headless testing in most web client environments.

Lighthouse

Google Lighthouse[12] is an automated page analysis tool which includes Accessibility, in addition to Performance, Progressive Web App standards, Best practices, and SEO. As shown in Figure 6-14, Lighthouse is built into the Chrome DevTools and can be accessed from the Audits tab.

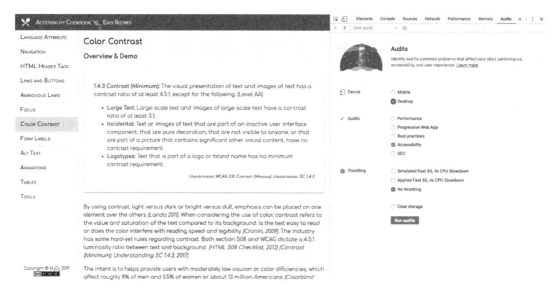

Figure 6-14. *Lighthouse in Chrome DevTools*

The Accessibility report in Figure 6-15 shows an accessibility score, and lists passes and failures, audits it didn't/couldn't perform, and suggestions for manual testing. Lighthouse is powered by axe but provides value in its convenient reporting, which can also be downloaded as JSON. When reviewing results manually, each item has a "Learn more" link which opens the same documentation page as the same link in axe.

---

[11]`www.deque.com/axe/integrations/`.

[12]`https://developers.google.com/web/tools/lighthouse/`.

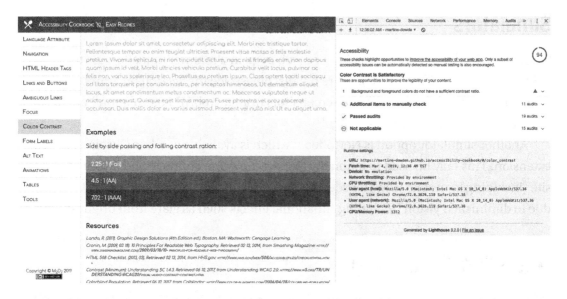

Figure 6-15. *Lighthouse audit results*

In addition to running the report manually, Lighthouse is available as a Node.js CLI which allows it to be scripted. Note that you will still need Chrome on the system that runs the script.

While the Lighthouse report and accessibility score are extremely valuable for scoping your accessibility project and providing an indicator of success, the big limitation is that it is tied directly to Chrome. For nearly all projects it will be important to perform testing in other browsers as well to ensure accessibility is universal and not specific to one device or browser.

Pa11y

Pa11y[13] is the name of the team, project, and set of open source tools for accessibility testing. It will be a good choice when your team is ready for Phase 3 or 4 and wants to put some work into automated accessibility testing. While Pa11y can be run successfully from the command line, it can also be integrated into a JavaScript or Node.js project for complete control over the automation. The report output can be in CSV or JSON for further processing. There is also a Dashboard[14] tool which is able to provide scheduled testing and show the status visually to your entire team.

---

[13]http://pa11y.org/.
[14]https://github.com/pa11y/pa11y-dashboard.

Simulators

Simulators display an altered version of a web page in a manner that attempts to simulate a specific disability. For more details, please see the section on Simulators in Chapter 3. In that section you'll see screenshots from a WebAIM Simulation[15] and a selection of simulations from Funkify.[16]

Another simulator option is NoCoffee,[17] which is available as a free Chrome browser extension. This may be used to manually inspect the color, contrast, and layout of a web site (including in mobile view) for scenarios where it may be extremely difficult to use due to diminished vision (including situational effects such as glare from bright sunlight).

Assistive Technology

The first chapter of this book included a section about Assistive Devices, Features, and Techniques. Please refer to that section for an overview of some available technology and how it can be used to support specific disabilities and circumstances. Here we will cover specific benefits of these technologies and the impact this may have on the development effort.

Screen Readers

Just like their name implies, Screen Readers convert text to audio by "reading" the content and structure of a web page. But they actually go a step further to making applications accessible to those who are unable to interact visually by providing sophisticated keyboard navigation for the content. Most screen readers are able to enable form completion, quickly skim the text on a page, and navigate by sections and paragraphs. Some also support additional forms of input and output such as braille and Optical Character Recognition (OCR).

The first time you use a screen reader without looking at the screen, you should begin to understand what is happening behind the scenes. All of the information that sighted users receive visually must have a structured nonvisual representation as well, so that the screen reader can provide the necessary context.

---

[15]https://webaim.org/simulations/.

[16]www.funkify.org/.

[17]https://accessgarage.wordpress.com/2013/02/09/458/.

When implementing accessibility on your web sites or web applications, it is important to understand how screen readers impact usability and your testing effort. In the same way that web developers understand the need to test various combinations of device, operating system, and browser, screen readers add an extra layer of complexity. The same screen reader may exhibit one set of behaviors when run through Firefox, but in another way when run through Chrome. Simply conforming to WCAG does not guarantee a good experience with a screen reader.

There are screen readers available for all major operating systems, and most systems come with at least one screen reader option pre-installed. Table 6-4 highlights some of the more common screen readers and where you may find them available.

Table 6-4. *Screen Readers*

Screen Reader	Platforms	URL	Free/Paid
JAWS	Windows	`www.freedomscientific.com/products/software/jaws/`	Paid
NVDA	Windows	`www.nvaccess.org/about-nvda/`	Free
Narrator	Windows	`https://support.microsoft.com/en-us/help/22798`	Free
VoiceOver	MacOS, iOS	`www.apple.com/accessibility/mac/vision/`	Free
ChromeVox	ChromeOS	`www.chromevox.com/`	Free
TalkBack	Android	`https://support.google.com/accessibility/android`	Free
ORCA	Linux	`https://help.gnome.org/users/orca/stable/`	Free

Adaptive Strategies

Many operating systems, including Windows and MacOS, have some built-in accessibility features intended to make a computer easier to use. Web browsers also have accessibility features available, either through settings or extensions. However, these features usually need to be specifically enabled by the user.

Sticky Keys is a feature which reduces the need for simultaneous key presses, but turning the SHIFT, CTRL, and ALT keys into toggle keys (similar to the Caps Lock and Num Lock keys).

Often **Magnification** is available, to expand one section of a screen to be much larger and more readable. Page **zoom** is supported by most web browsers as well, and often the default text size may be adjusted to be larger or smaller.

There are **High Contrast** color modes to help with text readability and with overall navigation within applications.

Mouse Keys, **Caret Browsing**, and similar features allow the pointer to be controlled using the keyboard arrow keys instead of a mouse or trackpad.

It will be important to understand which of these features, along with the many others available, are in use by your users while they are accessing your web site. Analytics will not provide this information, so you will need to interview or survey your users directly to gather this information.

These features may interact with other assistive technology or with the style sheets or JavaScript within your application in ways that render it unusable. Manual testing with these features should definitely be part of your accessibility practice, as your team and your company become more experienced.

Password Managers

While it is commonly understood how password managers improve personal security online, they may also be used as an accessibility tool. For example, a strong password, with suitable length and entropy, may be nearly impossible for users with cognitive, neurological, or visual limitations to read and type correctly. And as password length recommendations increase year after year, passwords become harder to remember. Add in the fact that every site has slightly different rules for what passwords are permitted, and the recommendation to use a unique password for every site, and quickly password managers become the only real option for most users to keep their credentials straight.

This means your web site or web application should avoid interfering with password managers. You should also test all forms in your application, including login, to be sure the the password manager works as intended. Some popular password managers as of this writing include LastPass,[18] 1Password,[19] and KeePass.[20]

---

[18]www.lastpass.com/.

[19]https://1password.com/.

[20]https://keepass.info/.

Resources

As wonderful as books are, the printed page remains fixed in time. While many of the concepts and ideas in this book should serve you well for years, technology changes at an incredible pace. Sooner or later you will find yourself wanting to learn more, keep up on the latest accessibility practices, or research some challenges you encounter. Some organizations and web sites are summarized in Table 6-5 that should serve you well in expanding your knowledge and continuing your education.

Table 6-5. *Accessibility Resources*

Organization	URL
AbilityNet	http://abilitynet.org.uk/
AFB	www.afb.org/
Service Manual	www.gov.uk/service-manual
The A11y Project	https://a11yproject.com/
Usability.gov	www.usability.gov/
W3C	www.w3.org/
WAI	www.w3.org/WAI/
WebAIM	https://webaim.org/

Web Accessibility In Mind (WebAIM) is a nonprofit organization from the Center for Persons with Disabilities at Utah State University.

The World Wide Web Consortium (W3C) and Web Accessibility Initiative (WAI) are covered in some depth in Chapter 2. The WAI publishes their own list of accessibility resources at www.w3.org/WAI/Resources/.

The American Foundation for the Blind (AFB) has a number of resources concerning assistive and accessible technology, focusing especially on resources for the visually impaired.

AbilityNet is a UK charity offering many resources, including training and technology, for accessibility at home, at work, and online.

Usability.gov is a government resource provided by the US Department of Health and Human Services (HHS). As a US government resource, it mostly provides guidance on Section 508 Standards. However, since Section 508 was updated in 2017 to align with WCAG 2.0, the resources here should be generally applicable.

Summary

In this chapter you have learned about a range of tools to help build accessible web sites and web applications, along with assistive technology that may need to interface with your software. Specifically, you're ready to

- Validate your application source files

- Explore your web site visually to check for issues and interactions

- Perform WCAG conformance testing of your web application

- Review usability and content delivery with screen readers

Index

A

a11y, 3
AbilityNet, 115
accessibility statement, 61–62, 83, 85
Accessibility-supported
    technologies, 30–31
Accessible Rich Internet Applications,
    see ARIA
Action plan, 80
Adaptive strategies, 13
Age related, 13
alternate flows, 63
alternate version, 30
American Foundation for the Blind
    (AFB), 38, 40, 115
analytics, 61, 86, 114
ARIA, 26–27, 38
Assistive technologies, 13
ATAG, 26
audio, 15
audit, 73, 87
Auditory, 5–6, 14
    hearing loss, 5
Authoring Tool Accessibility Guidelines,
    see ATAG

B

Berners-Lee, Tim, 1, 23, 38
braille, 14, 39

browser, 58, 68, 74, 103
Bush, Vannevar, 19

C

Captions, 14, 71
Caret Browsing, 114
CCD flatbed scanner, 36
Cerf, Sigrid, 35
Cerf, Vinton, 35
CERN, 23, 38
Chisholm, Wendy, 40
Cognitive, 9
    simulators, 48
Complete process, 30
Conformance, 28–29
Conforming Alternate Version, *see*
    alternate version
Content, 3, 17
continuous integration, 83, 87
Convention on the Rights of Persons with
    Disabilities, 2

D

developers, 45
disability, 4
Disability Discrimination
    Act 1992, 44
discoverability, 73

© Martine Dowden and Michael Dowden 2019
M. Dowden and M. Dowden, *Approachable Accessibility*, https://doi.org/10.1007/978-1-4842-4881-2

W

W3C, 1, 24, 39, 40, 115
WAI, 1, 24, 115
WAI-ARIA, *see* ARIA
WCAG, 26, 27, 40
    A, 29
    AA, 29
    AAA, 29
    documentation, 32
    guidelines, 27
    quick reference, 32
    success criteria, 27

Web Accessibility Initiative, *see* WAI
WebAIM, 40, 115
Web Content Accessibility Guidelines,
    see WCAG
Wonder, Stevie, 36
World Wide Web, 22, 38
World Wide Web Consortium, *see* W3C
Wright, Jesse, 37
WWW, *see* World Wide Web

X, Y, Z

Xerox, 36

Printed in the United States
By Bookmasters